Harvey Summ

EBTS does not necessarily
agree with all the views
expressed in this book.

The World's Most Popular Game

and Other Sermons

By

Monroe Parker, D.D., Ph.D.

Price $2.29

Sword of the Lord Publishers

Murfreesboro, Tennessee

Printed and bound in the United States of America

TABLE OF CONTENTS

FOREWORD

I am extremely happy to introduce this book of sermons by Dr. Monroe Parker whom I have known for more than three decades. I have heard Dr. Parker preach most of these sermons and under varied circumstances. Some I have heard in the spiritually heated hour of a great evangelistic campaign where many were being saved. Others I have heard in an atmosphere of Christian and fundamental intellectualism where Dr. Parker has preached to thousands of college students. Wherever they have been preached, the breath of God and heavenly anointing has been upon them.

Putting these messages in book form is certainly of God because sermons and preaching like this need to live on for future generations if Jesus tarries. These are more than sermons, they are sparks from God's anvil; they are coals of fire from His altar; they are flashing swords of truth from God's Book of truth. As the sermons of Moody, Torrey, Billy Sunday and others still live by printed page and are still bringing souls to Christ, so will the dynamic messages of Monroe Parker influence the generations yet to come.

Dr. Parker's ministry is unique in that he has been successful and productive in many fields. His evangelistic ministry has been one of the most outstanding of our time. His work as a college president and executive cannot be excelled. His pastoral work and great conference ministry are also the ministries of "a man sent from God." His sermons are the type of Bible messages which God uses in all these corners of His vineyard.

Since in the divine and sovereign plan of God, "it pleased

God by the foolishness of preaching to save them that believe" (I Cor. 1:21), how graciously blessed we are to have such strong, scripturally sane and tender sermons as those by Dr. Monroe Parker. Though these messages are scholarly, as Dr. Parker is a great scholar, they are plain and to the point so as to reach men and women for Christ from all walks of life.

Dr. Tom Malone

INTRODUCTION

Having had the high privilege and the awesome responsibility to lecture to thousands of ministerial students in a number of colleges and theological seminaries, and having been in evangelistic work for many years, the author has been repeatedly urged to put into print his evangelistic sermons.

From the hundreds of evangelistic sermons which he preaches those contained in this book have been selected because they are designed to evangelize the unsaved and edify those who are saved. Some of them have appeared with variations in THE SWORD OF THE LORD and other publications. "The World's Most Popular Game," "Prayer of Divine Passion," "Looking for a City," and "Death Takes No Holiday" have won prizes in SWORD Sermon Contests.

This book has been prepared and these sermons are being released with the prayer that in the reading of the sermons, as it has been in the preaching of them, it may please God to use them to His great glory and with the ultimate result of the salvation of many souls.

Monroe Parker

Dr. Monroe Parker

The World's Most Popular Game

"I have sinned: return, my son David: for I will no more do thee harm, because my soul was precious in thine eyes this day: behold, I have played the fool, and have erred exceedingly."—I Sam. 26:21.

The most popular game in the world is not necessarily played on the gridiron, the basketball court, the baseball field, the ice rink, or in the gymnasium. It may be played anywhere. It is a universal game and has been played in all ages.

Saul Played the Popular Game

Saul, the son of Kish, played this game three thousand years ago when he became inflated with pride, fell into sin, realized his folly and became jealous of David, who now held the esteem of his people, which he had so shamefully lost. David was fleeing from the jealous king and for the second time spared the king's life when he could easily have taken it. The first time Saul had stopped to rest in the mouth of a cave in the wilderness of En-gedi and David, who was concealed in the cave, cut the skirt from Saul's robe. Saul knew nothing of it until he had left the cave and David came out and called to him and showed him the skirt from his robe. Saul wept and confessed that he was wrong and that God's favor was with David. He conceded that David would become king and returned to his home.

David Spares Saul Again

Now Saul's jealousy had overcome him again and he was seeking David's life. He followed David into the wilderness of Ziph. Here he stopped for the night while Saul slept in a trench with Abner and his soldiers slept all around him. David stole into Saul's camp and took Saul's spear and a cruse of water that was by his side. He then went over on the hill across the valley and cried out, rebuking Abner and saying, "As the Lord liveth, ye are worthy to die, because ye have not kept your master, the Lord's anointed" (I Sam. 26:16).

When Saul realized that David had stood above him as he slept with spear in hand but that he had spared his life the second time, he said, "I have sinned: return, my son David: for I will no more do thee harm, because my soul was precious in thine eyes this day: behold, I have played the fool, and have erred exceedingly" (I Sam. 26:21).

"I have sinned....I have played the fool." That heart-rending cry has been ringing down the ages and every man, woman, boy, and girl who ever drew a breath of air, except our blessed Lord Jesus Christ, has at some time played the game of sin and thereby played the fool.

Playing the Fool Is Popular Play

First, the one who sins plays the fool. It is foolish to sin because sin is against God, against others, and against self.

Sin Is Against God

When David confessed his great sin to God he said, "Against thee, thee only, have I sinned, and done this evil in thy sight" (Ps. 51:4). Later in his prayer he declared that if he were restored to fellowship and blessing, he would teach transgressors the way of the Lord and sinners would be converted to Him. Others were affected not only by David's act of sin, but also by David's estrangement from God.

Sin has an effect upon the one who is playing the game. In David's case his joy was gone, his power was gone, and that awful sense of guilt overwhelmed his soul.

Sin Grieves God

To commit sin is foolish because it grieves God and robs Him of His glory. "Because that, when they knew God, they glorified him not as God, neither were thankful; but became vain in their imaginations, and their foolish heart was darkened. Professing themselves to be wise, they became fools, And changed the glory of the uncorruptible God into an image made like to corruptible man, and to birds, and four-footed beasts, and creeping things" (Rom. 1:21-23).

The sins of Saul brought grief to the Lord and to Samuel, His prophet. After Saul's disobedience in sparing Agag, the king of the Amalekites, we read, "And Samuel came no more to see Saul until the day of his death: nevertheless Samuel mourned for Saul: and the Lord repented that he had made Saul king over Israel" (I Sam. 15:35).

Sinner, you have no idea how your sins grieve the heart of God. Every sin of your life was upon Jesus Christ when He hanged on the cross of Calvary. And He felt the weight of it in His soul which had infinite capacity to suffer. Every oath, every dirty word, every lie, every hateful, unkind word spoken against the holy Trinity, or the Holy Bible, whether in an effort to destroy the true faith or to build up a false religion, dishonors Christ and grieves the great heart of God. Every effort to enthrone man in God's place is an effort to dethrone God.

Every act of aggression toward others or every wrong attitude toward others—theft, adultery, murder, lust, hate, false witness, or covetousness—is an act against God or a wrong attitude toward God. It is foolish to sin because it is against God and man is a fool to oppose the Almighty.

"Behold, I have sinned....I have played the fool," confessed the haughty king.

Sin Is Against Others

I talked with an old drunkard in the Evansville Rescue Mission in Evansville, Indiana, one night. He kept saying that his sins were not hurting anyone but himself. During the service he fell under conviction for his sins and responded to the invitation. Then he began to talk about how he had wronged his wife and children. He had left them ragged, cold, and hungry without a source of livelihood. You cannot sin without affecting others. The sins of Saul affected all of Israel. Saul's son, Jonathan, was not to reign in Saul's stead because of the sins of Saul. It is foolish to sin because it is against one's fellows and one is a fool to wrong the society of which he is a part, whether it be the home, the municipality, the state, or society in general.

Sin Is Against Self

It is foolish to sin because it is against one's self and one is a fool to injure himself. There is a law of spiritual harvest. "Whatsoever a man soweth, that shall he also reap. For he that soweth to his flesh shall of the flesh reap corruption" (Gal. 6:7,8).

When Saul was anointed king over Israel he was very humble. When lots were taken at Mizpah to determine who should be king and the lot fell to the family of Kish and then to Saul, they found Saul hidden among the stuff (I Sam. 10: 22). But after Saul had reigned two years he had become proud and self-willed. When he thought Samuel was late coming to Gilgal where they were to meet he arrogantly entered into the sanctuary usurping the authority of a priest and offered sacrifice.

Saul's Dynasty Rejected

When Saul told Samuel what he had done, Samuel said, "Thou hast done foolishly: thou hast not kept the commandment of the Lord thy God, which he commanded thee: for now would the Lord have established thy kingdom upon Israel for ever. But now thy kingdom shall not continue" (I Sam. 13:13,14).

Saul's sin affected the Lord; it affected Saul's family and

his kingdom and it affected himself. Saul played the fool when he intruded into the office of the priest because "the way of a fool is right in his own eyes" (Prov. 12:15); he played the fool because "a fool's wrath is presently known" (Prov. 12:16) and "anger resteth in the bosom of fools" (Eccles. 7:9) in his failure to give obedience to God's command to utterly slay the Amalekites. Following this an evil spirit from the Lord troubled him so that his servants brought David to play his harp and soothe his nerves on these occasions. "There is no peace, saith my God, to the wicked" (Isa. 57:21). Saul lost his kingdom, his family, his peace, his glory, his power, his fellowship with Samuel, the man of God, his guidance and his life on account of his sins.

"Fools make a mock of sin" (Prov. 14:9), but this is a popular game. "It is as sport to a fool to do mischief" (Prov. 10:23) and "a fool layeth open his folly" (Prov. 13:16). "The heart of fools is in the house of mirth" (Eccles. 7:4).

Reflex Effect of Sin

Sin has a reflex effect upon those who engage in it. This is seen in the first chapter of Romans where we read that those who professed themselves to be wise and "became fools and changed the glory of God" were given up by God to receive in themselves "that recompense of their error which was meet." It is foolish to sin because sin injures one's self and one is a fool to injure himself.

Second, the man who builds without a foundation plays the fool. Fools build their character on a foundation of sand. Jesus said, "Therefore whosoever heareth these sayings of mine, and doeth them, I will liken him unto a wise man, which built his house upon a rock: And the rain descended, and the floods came, and the winds blew, and beat upon that house; and it fell not: for it was founded upon a rock. And every one that heareth these sayings of mine, and doeth them not, shall be likened unto a foolish man, which built his house upon the sand: And the rain descended, and the floods came, and the winds blew, and beat upon that house; and it fell: and great was the fall of it" (Matt. 7:24-27).

How foolish to build without a solid foundation! But that is what is being done in the modern educational system. Some time ago the late Dorothy Thompson related the frank confessions of four college graduates concerning the effects of education on their lives. All were graduated from an old and honored eastern institution. All four had achieved high scholastic records and had won other honors. While the four were all very different from each other, yet each told substantially the same distressing story.

They testified that their education had broken down their belief in positive values; it had weakened their faith in their country and its traditions; it had left them in intellectual confusion and inner despair. They had sought an escape in various ways: one cast his lot temporarily with the Communists; another into complete skepticism and cynicism; another into "the only thing that seemed solid—his own egotism and self-interest."

One boy, who came near to a nervous breakdown and whose family sent him to a psychiatrist before he managed to pull himself together, said, "When I went to college I was full of enthusiasm, particularly interested in history and philosophy. I wanted to find out what made the wheels go around in the world. I wanted to prepare myself to do something—not just make money. I wanted to love something—something bigger than I am—but by my junior year I had become convinced that there wasn't anything that could be believed. Everything was relative, and I was in space. I was like the guy in that poem of Gillett Burgess's:

> I wish that my room had a floor.
> I don't much care for a door.
> But this floating around
> Without touching the ground
> Is getting to be quite a bore.

We need to educate our young people but we must give them a solid foundation to stand on.

The Fool Leaves God Out

The fool leaves God out of his life. "The fool hath said in his heart, There is no God" (Ps. 53:1). In his head the fool knows that there is a God. The fact of God is an institution. Man knows instinctively and by intuition that there is a God. But "in his heart" the fool says, "No God." The words "there is" are in italics; they are not in the original Hebrew. The fool says, "No God"—that is, "No God for me."

Many people who are not atheists theoretically are practical atheists. An atheist orator on a soapbox said, "There is no God." A good old Christian man at the edge of the crowd said, "He means that he knows uv." There are a lot of practical atheists like the rich fool who "thought within himself" but left God out of his thinking.

God has a will concerning everything in your life. He has a will about where you go to school, whom you marry, where you live, how you make a living, how you conduct yourself every moment. God has a blueprint for your life and if you are trying to improve on God's plan for your life you are playing the fool.

Third, the person who puts off the most important thing in his life—salvation—and gambles with his immortal soul, plays the fool. If you gain the whole world and lose your soul you make a poor bargain. You are a fool to trade "an inheritance incorruptible, and undefiled, and that fadeth not away" for an effort to gain this godless world which no man has ever gained. If you should succeed in gaining the world, it would bring you only one disappointment after another. Then if you *could* gain the world, you could not keep it. You will have to die. And if you did not have to die you could not keep the world because some day God will destroy it.

No Lease on Life

"It is appointed unto men once to die" (Heb. 9:27). "Ye shall die like men" (Ps. 82:7). You have no lease on life. It is foolish to put off salvation. This message could be your last warning. Jesus said that the five virgins who were unprepared were foolish virgins. He also told about a man who said to his soul, "Thou hast much goods laid up for many years," but He said that God said unto that man, "Thou fool, this night thy soul shall be required of thee." He was a fool because he thought he had plenty of time.

A Foolish Old Man

The man who puts off the most important matter of life is foolish. I talked with an old man about his need of Christ one night. He said to me, "I heard the Gospel before you were born." I replied, "Then you have put off salvation for a long time. This could be your last call." He said, "Don't worry about me. I know the Gospel. I will be saved before I die, but I am not ready to do it now." I answered with the Bible, "Boast not thyself of to morrow; for thou knowest not what a day may bring forth" (Prov. 27:1). The man became angry and refused to talk. But he died that night at 2 o'clock and went out into a Christless eternity.

Calling Late

In a North Carolina town where I held meetings a man fell from a three-hundred-foot smokestack. On the way to the ground he cried so that he was heard over a mile away, "Lord, have mercy on my soul!" If he cried in faith his soul bounced right on back to Heaven, for the Bible tells us, "For whosoever shall call upon the name of the Lord shall be saved" (Rom. 10:13). If the man did not call in faith, he kept on going. A man is taking a long chance to put off calling upon God until he is dying. It is a foolish thing to do.

Jesus Knocks At the Door

Oh, how foolish is the mind of man! "The foolishness of God is wiser than men" (I Cor. 1:25). I am free to confess that I was a fool indeed because I turned Jesus away from my heart's door often before that memorable day when, praise God, I let Him come in. He knocked one day, and I said, "Who is there?" He said, "Jesus." I asked, "What do You want, Jesus?" He said, "I want to come in and set things right!" I said, "No, You will spoil my plans and You will kill my joy." My plans needed changing and my joy was empty, but I turned Jesus away. He came back one day and knocked again. I asked, "Who is there?" He answered, "Jesus." "What do You want, Jesus?" "I want to come in and bring salvation to you," He said. But I sent Him away. Then one day He knocked again and I let Him come in. Thank God! I let Him come in.

> He stood at my heart's door in sunshine
> and rain,
> And patiently waited an entrance to gain;
> What shame that so long He entreated in
> vain,
> For He is so precious to me.

Just now the Lord Jesus Christ is knocking at your heart's door. He loved you and gave Himself for you. He took all of your sins in His body and died on a cross to pay your penalty of guilt. He now lives and is able to save. "He that hath the Son hath life; and he that hath not the Son of God hath not life" (I John 5:12).

Surely you will not play the fool! Do not go on without Jesus, friend. Do not be so foolish. Open your heart to the risen Christ!

II

The Great Paradox

Let us begin to read in Matthew, chapter 27, beginning at verse 38 and read through verse 44. The text is a portion of verse 42.

"Then were there two thieves crucified with him, one on the right hand, and another on the left. And they that passed by reviled him, wagging their heads, And saying, Thou that destroyest the temple, and buildest it in three days, save thyself. If thou be the Son of God, come down from the cross. Likewise also the chief priests mocking him, with the scribes and elders, said, He saved others; himself he cannot save. If he be the King of Israel, let him now come down from the cross, and we will believe him. He trusted in God; let him deliver him now, if he will have him: for he said, I am the Son of God."—Matt. 27:38-44.

I call your special attention to this portion of verse 42, "He saved others; himself he cannot save." While this was spoken in sarcasm and in derision, it was in a sense a true statement.

The Scene

It was an awful scene. The Lord of Glory had been nailed to a wooden cross and He hanged there on a hill called Calvary which means cranium. The top of this small mountain a short distance north of the city of Jerusalem is in the shape of a skull. Its face is toward the city. There are two small caves forming eye sockets with a limestone nose bridge between. Chemical tests have shown that the upper crust of that hill known as "Gordon's Calvary" is composed of human bones.

Place of Shame

It was here in this place of ignominy that He was forced to bring His cross. His face had been beaten until it had become a swollen mass. "His visage was so marred more than any man, and his form more than the sons of men" (Isa. 52:14). He had given His "back to the smiters," and His "cheeks to them that pluck off the hair." He had not hidden His "face from shame and spitting" (Isa. 50:6). His back had been scourged to purple ribbons; He had been stripped of His clothing and forced to lie down upon that hard, rough, wooden cross He had borne up the mountainside. Cruel nails had been driven through His hands and the cross had been raised and then His feet had been spiked securely to the wood. Writhing in awful agony He hanged there naked and bleeding as wicked men laughed and jeered and wagged their heads and shot out their lips in derision.

The Challenge

Could He not accept that challenge? He is the infinite God. "By him all things consist" (Col. 1:17). Even the elements that compose that cross and the nails are held together by Him. Let Him prove His deity! He had said, "Therefore doth my Father love me, because I lay down my life, that I might take it again. No man taketh it from me, but I lay it down of myself. I have power to lay it down, and I have power to take it again" (John 10:17,18).

They cannot take His life from Him. Let Him prove it. Can He not accept the challenge, "Come down from the cross!"? He is the infinite God! Let Him prove His deity! But, no. He came to die on that cross. He had said, "The Son of man must suffer many things, and be rejected of the elders and chief priests and scribes, and be slain, and be raised the third day" (Luke 9:22). This was in the eternal counsel of God and was necessary.

I. THE BITTER CUP

If He were to save others He could not save Himself. He had to drink the bitter cup the Father gave Him, for He was the obedient Servant. Matthew gives the account of three prayers Jesus prayed in the Garden of Gethsemane.

1. "O my Father, if it be possible, let this cup pass from me: nevertheless not as I will, but as thou wilt."—Matt. 26:39.

2. "O my Father, if this cup may not pass away from me, except I drink it, thy will be done."—Matt. 26:42.

3. "And he left them, and went away again, and prayed the third time, saying the same words."—Matt. 26:44.

In Hebrews 5:7 we read that when He offered up supplications "with strong crying and tears" He was heard. His prayer, "not as I will, but as thou wilt" was heard and "Though he were a Son, yet learned he obedience by the things which he suffered" (Heb. 5:8). His prayer was for the Father's will to be done, so when Simon Peter cut off the right ear of Malchus, the servant of the high priest, Jesus said "unto Peter, Put up thy sword into the sheath: the cup which my Father hath given me, shall I not drink it?"

Jesus Had to Drink the Cup

In the will of the Father Jesus had to drink the cup. He could not come down from the cross. If He were to save others He could not save Himself.

II. HE SAVED OTHERS

There is no doubt that He saved others. He came for that purpose. "This is a faithful saying, and worthy of all acceptation, that Christ Jesus came into the world to save sinners" (I Tim. 1:15).

A. Before He Came

All through the days of the Old Testament the finger of prophecy pointed to the coming of a Saviour. Before He was born of the virgin in Bethlehem the angel of the Lord appeared to Joseph in a dream and said, "Joseph, thou son of David, fear not to take unto thee Mary thy wife: for that which is conceived in her is of the Holy Ghost. And she shall bring forth a son, and thou shalt call his name JESUS: for he shall save his people from their sins" (Matt. 1:20,21).

B. While He Was Here

When Jesus came He claimed to be the Saviour. On one occasion He said, "For the Son of man is come to save that which was lost" (Matt. 18:11). Again He said, "For the Son of man is come to seek and to save that which was lost" (Luke 19:10).

He Verified His Claim

He not only claimed that He could save people from their sins but He also verified His claims. In Capernaum "they brought to him a man sick of the palsy, lying on a bed" (Matt. 9:2). Jesus said to the man, "Son, be of good cheer; thy sins be forgiven thee" (Matt. 9:2). Some of the scribes began to reason within themselves, "This man blasphemeth." Jesus, knowing what they were thinking, said to them, "But that ye may know that the Son of man hath power [authority] on earth to forgive sins, (then saith he to the sick of the palsy) Arise, take up thy bed, and go unto thine house. And he arose, and departed to his house" (Matt. 9:6,7). Jesus could say not only, "Thy sins be forgiven thee," but He could also prove that He spoke with authority by following the statement with the command, "Arise, take up thy bed, and go unto thine house."

Miracles Established Authority

Such miracles were given to prove authority. For instance, at the bush when Moses expressed concern that the people might not believe that Jehovah had sent him, God told him to cast his rod on the ground. Moses obeyed and the rod became a serpent. God told him to take the serpent by the tail. When Moses obeyed, the serpent became a rod in his hand. God told him to go to Egypt and tell his people that Jehovah had sent him. This miracle would be performed "that they may believe that the Lord God of their fathers, the God of Abraham, the God of Isaac, and the God of Jacob, hath appeared unto thee" (Exod. 4:5). We have no need of such miracles today because we have a completed Bible which was given by those whose commissions were sealed and proven by miracles, the prophets and the apostles.

Prophesies and Tongues

One of the earlier epistles was I Corinthians. In this epistle Paul wrote, "Charity never faileth: but whether there be prophecies, they shall fail; whether there be tongues, they shall cease; whether there be knowledge, it shall vanish away. For we know in part, and we prophesy in part. But when that which is perfect [complete] is come, then that which is in part shall be done away" (I Cor. 13:8-10).

When Paul said, "Whether there be prophecies, they shall fail," he did not mean that a prophecy given by God would fail to come to pass. He meant this: "Here is a man with the gift of prophecy. The Word of God is completed; his gift fails him, at least the predictive element of that gift." We have a complete revelation, "a more sure word of prophecy" proven by miracles of old. When Paul said, "Whether there be tongues, they shall cease," he meant that when the Word of God was completed it would be a perfect revelation and no longer would we need such demonstrations as that which took place at Pentecost. Miracles prove authority, so when Jesus told the palsied man that his sins were forgiven He proved His authority to forgive sins by performing a miracle.

Blind Man Saved

Jesus said to a blind man near the city of Jericho, "Receive thy sight: thy faith hath saved thee." They who beheld the miracle "gave praise unto God" (Luke 18:42,43). Jesus could say not only, "Thy faith hath saved thee," but He could also say, "Receive thy sight."

Zacchaeus

Zacchaeus of Jericho was not just an ordinary sinner. He was "chief among the publicans" of Jericho. But when Jesus came into his life he stood and said to Jesus, "Behold, Lord, the half of my goods I give to the poor; and if I have taken any thing from any man by false accusation, I restore him fourfold" (Luke 19:8). Here is proof of the fact that a great change took place in the life of Zacchaeus. This man who had spent his life in greed and lust taking money by false accusation was willing not only to make restitution according to the Levitical law, but he also became a benevolent soul giving half of his goods to the poor. Jesus said, "This day is salvation come to this house" (Luke 19:9). For three years Jesus went about preaching, teaching, performing miracles and saving souls.

While He Was Dying

At the very time they were scornfully jeering, "He saved others, himself he cannot save," He was saving souls. Not only was He dying for the sins of all the people who have ever been saved or ever shall be saved, but He was also saving individuals. There was a man on a cross nearby who, according to his own testimony, was not fit to live in this world, one who deserved capital punishment, who said to his companion on the other side of Jesus, "We receive the due reward of our deeds" (Luke 23:41). But that day before the sun went down Jesus entered Paradise with the soul of that repentant thief.

C. After He Arose

"He saved others" after He arose from the dead, millions
of others. There was Saul of Tarsus. He was on his way to
Damascus with papers from the high priest giving him authority to persecute Christians. He had just left Jerusalem
where he was consenting to the death of Stephen. He was
breathing out threatenings and cursings against the Christians when suddenly a shaft of light brighter than the noon-
day sun shone upon him, putting out his sight and casting
him to the ground, and a loud voice cried out to him, "Saul,
Saul, why persecutest thou me?" He answered, "Who art
thou, Lord?" There has never been a more instantaneous
conversion and dedication. "Who art thou, *Lord*?" The
VOICE answered, "I am Jesus whom thou persecutest."

Become an Apostle

At the command of the Lord the blinded Saul arose and
went on to Damascus where, through a miracle, he received
his sight and after three years in the Arabian desert studying the Old Testament in the light of this wonderful, new
revelation, he became Paul, the great apostle, the bond-
slave of Christ whose one device is bannered forth in his
excellent cry, "For to me to live is Christ."

Millions of Others

Jesus saved millions of others. He saved my poor soul.
If all the proof I had that Jesus is a Saviour was what He has
done for me, that would be all I would need. Only God could
do for one what Jesus Christ has done for me.

Mel Trotter

Only God could have done what Jesus did for the late Mel
Trotter. Mel Trotter was a drunkard. He staggered home
one night and found his wife wringing her hands in distrac-
tion. She said, "Mel, the baby is dying. The doctor just
left and he left this prescription. Mel, do you understand?

Take this prescription and go to a drugstore and get it filled.
Here is 60¢. It is all we have. Be careful, Mel. Surely
some druggist will let you have the medicine." Mel Trotter
took that money and on his way to the drugstore he turned
into a saloon and spent the money for drink. That night
when he staggered back home he found his wife clutching in
her arms the lifeless form of a dead baby. The next day
when they interred the little body Mel Trotter was in a saloon drunk from liquor he obtained by selling some of the
possessions of the little babe as it lay in its little coffin.
He used to tell that he was even tempted to take the shoes
from its little feet and sell them to buy drink. He did not
yield to this temptation and he resented the fact that it was
told that he did this although he said he was tempted to do
so. In that condition he said, "I am not fit to live. I am
going to end my life." He had heard that a man committed
suicide by jumping into soft concrete at a place where they
were building a bridge in South Chicago. He started down to
the southside to follow the man's example. On his way he
came to the old Pacific Garden Mission, the place where
Billy Sunday was converted. A gang of his old cronies were
around the door. One of them said, "Mel, you seem nervous. Let's go inside. That's the place for you," and pushed
him in the door. Mel stood in the back as they sang, "There
is a fountain filled with blood drawn from Emmanuel's
veins. And sinners plunged beneath that flood lose all their
guilty stains." He was fat and bloated and had a red nose.
Harry Monroe, who with "Mother Clark" led Billy Sunday to
Christ, saw him back there. He went back and buttonholed
him and said, "Come on, Fatty. Christ will save you," as
he led him to the penitent form. I heard Mr. Trotter tell
the story. He said, "That night at twenty-five minutes past
nine I passed out of death into life and out of darkness into
light." Mel Trotter became one of the most elegant Christian gentlemen I have ever known. He founded sixty-three
Gospel missions in America and led thousands to Christ.

The last time I saw him was in the Battery Park Hotel in Asheville, North Carolina, not long before he died. He put his arm around me and said, "Mon, old boy, for me the outlook is dark but the uplook is bright."

Transforming Power of Christ

I have known drunkards to quit their drink without Jesus Christ and I have known other sinners to reform without Him, but I have never known lives so transformed by any other power on earth as those I have observed who trust in Him.

III. GREATEST WORK IN THE WORLD

"He saved others." That is the greatest work in all the world, saving others. That is God's work. Only God can save others. Yet it is the work of Christ, the Son. Only Christ can save. His blood was essential. Only the Father can save. Only the Son can save. Only the Holy Spirit can save. 'No man cometh to the Father except the Spirit draw him.'

We May Save Others

There is a sense in which only the Father can save. There is a sense in which only the Son can save. There is a sense in which only the Spirit can save. And there is a sense in which you and I may save others. "Let him know, that he which converteth the sinner from the error of his way shall save a soul from death, and shall hide a multitude of sins" (Jas. 5:20).

Shouting Ground

Some years ago I was in a meeting at the Temple Baptist Church in Saint Paul, Minnesota, where we had a blessed revival with many souls. Several years later I was there again. A fine looking young man came and spoke to me and asked, "Do you know me?" I said, "I know your face but I cannot recall your name." He said, "You ought to know.

You saved me. And I have been called to preach." I answered, "Son, I did not save you. Jesus saved you." He said, "I know that but you told me about Jesus so you saved me, too." As I left the church I began to think of what that young man said and the Holy Spirit brought to my mind the last verse of James, "...he which converteth the sinner from the error of his way shall save a soul from death...." I got on shouting ground. I said, "Praise God! I am a saviour! 1 have saved an immortal soul! I have snatched a brand from the burning. I have had the joy of saving thousands of souls!"

Crown of Joy

I do not wonder that God has offered a "crown of joy" to the soul winner. There is no joy comparable to the joy of winning a soul to Jesus Christ. Daniel said, "They that be wise shall shine as the brightness of the firmament; and they that turn many to righteousness as the stars for ever and ever" (Dan. 12:3).

It is a great privilege to be a soul winner. It is a privilege the angels covet. I believe the angels would be glad to leave their high estate and come down into this old world of sin and woe to "suffer the slings and arrows of outrageous fortune...that flesh is heir to" if they might have the privilege of winning souls.

A Bounden Duty

But, my friends, it is not only a great privilege and joy to win souls; it is a responsibility and a duty we cannot afford to shirk. Jesus gave the Great Commission to His disciples and first church at Jerusalem and that commission is resting incumbent upon every church of the Lord Jesus Christ today, and it is resting upon every individual Christian. None is excluded. "Ye shall be witnesses unto me." "Ye" is plural. It means "Y'all" to you Southerners and "Youse" to you Yankees.

Spiritual Manslaughter

I was in a revival in Detroit and a man asked me to go to county prison and talk with a relative of his who was sentenced for manslaughter. I went down to the prison and led the man to Christ. I had him to sign his name to one of Dr. Bob Jones' little gospel tracts, *This Is Important*, that has a footnote with a blank for one to sign the statement, "I hereby accept the Lord Jesus Christ as my Saviour." The man asked me to send the tract to his mother who he said was a Christian. That man was in prison three years for manslaughter, not first degree murder. He had been left in charge of a railroad gate. He failed to put the gate down when a train was coming. A car ran onto the track and a man was killed. So he was doing time for the dereliction of duty. I left the prison that day asking this question, "Lord, is it so that if I fail to put down the gate of warning and people run past me into Hell I become guilty of spiritual manslaughter?" The Holy Spirit brought to my mind this verse of Scripture found in two places in Ezekiel 3:18 and 33:8— "When I say unto the wicked, O wicked man, thou shalt surely die; if thou dost not speak to warn the wicked from his way, that wicked man shall die in his iniquity; but his blood will I require at thine hand." Notice: not "thy blood," but "his blood...at thine hand."

The Extent of Responsibility

Someone may ask, "Where does my responsibility end? I could spend every working hour going from house to house. I could buttonhole people on the street, and I could stand on the corner and cry for people to repent and turn to God. Does God want me to do that?"

Rowland Hill

God may raise up someone like Rowland Hill with that kind of ministry. He stood preaching on the street. People called him a fanatic and suggested that he confine his preaching to Sunday and to the churchhouse. Rowland Hill said, "Coming here today I passed a gravel pit where men were working and I saw the gravel begin to slide. I yelled to the top of my voice, 'Get out of the pit! Get out of the pit!' Some of the men responded but others were caught in the slide. Again I yelled, 'Bring your shovels!' Men working in another quarry nearby rushed to the rescue. They uncovered the men and they lived. Nobody called me a fanatic. Now I stand to warn you of eternal damnation and some call me a fanatic." Rowland Hill stopped the Royal Procession in England and auctioned the soul of the queen. When the guards would have taken him away the queen ordered him released and listened to his message and made her decision to receive Christ.

John Vassar

God may raise up a Rowland Hill or a John Vassar. Old John Vassar stopped people everywhere he went and spoke to them about their souls. Once he led a woman to Christ in a hotel lobby while she waited for her husband. When her husband arrived he found his wife in tears of joy. He asked, "What's wrong, dear?" She said, "An old man just talked to me about my soul." The husband said, "Why did you not tell him to mind his own business?" She answered, "If you had seen that old man you would have known that he was minding his business." I say God may raise up a Rowland Hill or a John Vassar but He wants us all to be sensitive to the prompting of His Spirit so we may be used according to His will.

He Will Lead You

I read of a man who passed thousands of people on the streets in Chicago. Suddenly he was impressed to speak to a man about his soul. The man was deeply under conviction and had left a gospel service. He told the man how to become a Christian and he went back with him to the service where he made a public profession of faith in Christ. The secret of success in soul winning is to be led by the Holy Spirit.

Filled With the Spirit

To be filled with the Spirit for soul winning empty your heart of everything that would grieve Him and ask Him to fill, lead, guide and teach you to win souls. Then in faith witness, obey the Lord and "go." He said, "Go...and preach the Gospel...and, lo, I am with you...." The "lo, I am with you" is contingent upon the "go." "Go" and "lo"!

The Word of God

Now, of course, the Word of God is the message we preach and there are cardinal truths easily understood which you must know in order to win souls. Surely you must know the plan of salvation, but you do not need to be a theological professor. I heard Dr. Lee Roberson, pastor of the great Highland Park Baptist Church, Chattanooga, Tennessee, tell about a man in that church who in one year won two hundred and seventy-six people to Christ and got them baptized in the Highland Park Baptist Church. There is no telling how many others he won to Christ whom he did not get into the church. That man is a layman who drives a linen supply truck and delivers towels to barber shops. Dr. Roberson said, "He has never had a course in soul winning." Then he facetiously said, "I am not going to let him take one, either."

Find a Way

The trouble with the average Christian is not that he does not know how to win souls. He is just not willing to pay the price. If you really care about getting souls to Christ you will find a way to do it.

IV. HE COULD NOT SAVE HIMSELF

Jesus saved others even though it meant that He could not

save Himself. And if you save others you cannot save yourself. Everything in this world worthwhile comes as the result of a sacrifice. Strike a match. If it gives off its light
and heat it must burn away. Light a candle. If it sheds its
light it must melt. We illuminate with electricity but this
calls for sacrifice. Great power dams are built at tremendous cost, or great power plants are erected and men must
go into the bowels of the earth and dig the coal to produce
the steam to turn the turbines that generate the electricity.
You have an education but you had to study and no matter
how brilliant you are you have had to engage in some meas-
ure of concentration.

We have this grand civilization—America, "the land of the
free, and the home of the brave." But our forefathers
braved stormy and uncharted seas to reach these shores.
The settlers endured the rigors of hunger and cold and heat
and epidemic and massacre and privation. Our men have
fought on the battlefields and in the air and on the sea and
under the sea in order that we might enjoy the great privi-
leges we have. Everything worthwhile is the result of sacrifice. Someone says, "But Jesus paid it all. Salvation is
free." Yes, but Paul said, I "fill up that which is behind in
the afflictions of Christ." Someone has said, "A story needs
a teller." The evangel needs an evangelist.

System of Paradoxes

Someone says, "If I have to sacrifice to save others I am
not going to do it. I am going to save myself." No, you are
not going to save yourself. You cannot save yourself. You
see, Christianity is a system of paradoxes. The way up is
down. "And whosoever shall exalt himself shall be abased;
and he that shall humble himself shall be exalted" (Matt: 23:
12). The way to live is to die.

> I lay in dust life's glory dead,
> And from the ground there blossoms red
> Life that shall endless be.

The way to be first is to put yourself last. Jesus said, "But many that are first shall be last; and the last first."

The First Last

One time I had some children on a picnic. When they lined up to get their food one big boy pushed a little girl out of the way at the front of the line and she fell on the ground. I helped her up and helped her brush the dirt off her dress. I told her to stop crying, that I would see that she got plenty to eat. The children were all lined up with the roughest boy in the crowd at the front of the line, the second roughest second in line, the third roughest third, etc. I asked, "Is everybody ready?" The little roughneck at the front of the line said, "Yeah. We are ready!" I said, "All right, we will pray and after prayer you will all wait until I give the signal to start." After we had the blessing I said, "If anybody gets out of place he will have to wait until everyone else has eaten. Now I want you to turn around right where you are and we will start at the other end of the line." The little girl was first and the bully who had pushed her down was last.

You know, God runs His program like that. Some fellow says, "I will be first." And somebody says, "Be sure to elect him as chairman. He won't cooperate if he can't run the thing." He thinks he is leading. Now, if God puts you first, you lead. Lead like a soldier, like the little girl I put first in line. But somebody puts himself first. He elbows everybody else out of the way and thinks he is leading. He marches right on up to the pearly gate. He stands there and waits for the gate to open. He has his nose against the pearl. After a while he looks at his watch and says, "I thought they would open on time up here." After a while things get so quiet he wonders what is the matter. He turns around and finds that he is standing there by himself. You know, there are twelve gates up there. They are all going in another gate and he will be the last one in. He has to run to make it.

Cannot Save Self

You cannot save yourself without giving yourself. "For whosoever will save his life shall lose it: and whosoever will lose his life for my sake shall find it" (Matt. 16:25).

One dry springtime when the valley had enjoyed no refreshing showers a little mountain streamlet ran through the valley on the way to the river. An old pond in the valley tipped its white cap and said, "Good morning, little stream! Where are you rushing in such a hurry?" The little stream answered, "Good morning, Old Pond! I am running down to the river to take the water that God has given me." "Ah," said the pond, "you are a foolish little creek. You will not find me giving mine away. The river will pour it in the ocean and the ocean doesn't need it, you know. We have had a dry spring and it will be a hot summer. I am going to keep all the water I can get." The little stream paid no attention to the selfish old pond. It just went singing and splashing and gurgling and laughing over the rocks and by the grassy knolls on down to the river to take the water God had given it. What about the old pond? Sure enough, they had a hot, dry summer in the valley. The old pond put his greedy arms around the water and held it tight, but it grew stagnant and bred mosquitoes. The frogs cast their venom on its bosom. Scum appeared over its face. The cattle found it stale and would not drink. Its fish began to die and after a while God smote it with a hotter breath and dried it up from the face of the earth. What about the little stream? It took its water out to the river. The river took it out to the sea. The sea sent it up in its purified incense to greet the skies. The winds like rushing steeds carried the great clouds to the mountaintops. God spoke and down came the mighty torrents and filled the stream to the full. As it ran down through the valley where the old pond used to be it sang, "Old ponds may come and old ponds may go, but I run on forever."

Dividends Forever

You cannot beat God giving. Every gift you place on the altar brings back so many blessings in its place that you haven't given anything. You have not sacrificed. You have made an investment that will bring forth dividends forever.

Back to Calvary

Let us go back to Calvary! Sure enough, He had to die. He could not save Himself. He cried, "It is finished." Then He said, "Father, into thy hands I commend my spirit." He bowed His head and gave up the ghost. The King of Kings and Lord of Lords was dead. They took Him down and prepared Him for burial. His body was limp and lifeless. They wrapped it in graveclothes and placed it in a borrowed tomb. But when three days had passed He made a laughingstock out of Hell. They laughed at Him as He hanged on the cross, but the Apostle Paul said, "And having spoiled principalities and powers, he made a show of them openly, triumphing over them in it" (Col. 2:15). In His resurrection He triumphed, and in Revelation we hear the mighty throng in Heaven crying, "Worthy is the Lamb that was slain to receive power, and riches, and wisdom, and strength, and honour, and glory, and blessing" (Rev. 5:12). My friends, in giving we gain!

III

To the Wise and the Unwise

I invite your attention to Romans, chapter 1, verse 14. "I am a debtor both to the Greeks, and to the Barbarians; both to the wise, and to the unwise" (Rom. 1:14).

This text sets forth the attitude of a humble, Spirit-filled man, a man of culture and scholarly background, a grateful man as he looked upon the sin-benighted world and faced the challenge of its needs. That was in a day when Rome was at the zenith of her power, when old cultures were shifting, when the art and philosophy and poetry of the Greeks were being amalgamated with the pragmatism and power of Roman imperialism.

The World Formidable

The world Paul faced was formidable and the Gospel he preached was 'foolishness to the Greeks and a stumbling block to the Jews.' The odds were against him and if he had been like most men he would have gone back to Antioch and started a tent factory and got rich. Then he could have written a book on *God and I Run Each Other's Business*. Or he would have gone back and found John Mark and they would have gone about and shown color slides on "The Beauties of Cyprus."

Gratitude

But Paul had something in him that would not let him turn back. He had gratitude—the gratitude through which the Spirit prompted him to write in chapter 12 of this same epistle:

"I beseech you therefore, brethren, by the mercies of

God, that ye present your bodies a living sacrifice, holy,
acceptable unto God, which is your reasonable service. And
be not conformed to this world: but be ye transformed by
the renewing of your mind, that ye may prove what is that
good, and acceptable, and perfect, will of God."—Rom. 12:
1,2.

The late Dr. Bob Jones, Sr., said, "Gratitude is one of the
loveliest flowers that blooms in the garden of the human
heart, and when that flower withers and dies in the heart of
any man that man is well nigh hopeless." In this chapter
Paul says of the heathen, "When they knew God, they glorified him not as God, *neither were thankful;* but became vain
in their imaginations, and their foolish heart was darkened"
(Rom. 1:21). But Paul was a grateful man. He was so grateful that he considered himself a debtor to all men as well as
to the Lord.

"O God," I cried, "why may I not forget?
These halt and hurt in life's hard battle throng me yet.
Am I their keeper? Am I to suffer for their sin?
Would that mine eyes had never been opened then."

The thorn-crowned and patient One replied,
"They thronged Me, too. I, too, have seen."
"Thy other children go at will," I said, protesting still.
"They go unheeding. But these halt, these hurt,
Yea, those that sin drag at my heart.
Why is it, Lord? I have tried!" '

He turned and looked at me, "But I have died."
"O God," I said, "I brought not forth this host
Of needy creatures, struggling, tempest-tossed.
They are not mine." He looked at them the look
Of one divine, then turned and looked at me,
"But they are Mine."

"O God," I said, "I understand at last.
I will henceforth bond-slave be.

To the weakest, vilest ones I will not more be free.''
He smiled and said, "It is for Me."
                              —R. E. Neighbour

I. SALVATION

Now in the first place, Paul regarded himself a debtor to all men because God had deigned to save his soul. Writing to the Corinthians the apostle said, "Ye are not your own, For ye are bought with a price" (I Cor. 6:19,20). Christian, you are a debtor because of your salvation. Think what Christ has done for you! Without Him there is no joy, nor peace, nor hope, nor way, nor truth, nor life. Without Him there is no satisfying joy. Sinner, "Do you want joy, real joy, wonderful joy? Let Jesus come into your heart!" In the eighth chapter of Acts we read about a great revival in Samaria under the leadership of Philip, the evangelist, and we read that "there was great joy in that city."

David cried unto the Lord, "in thy presence is fullness of joy" (Ps. 16:11). Peter wrote of Jesus, "Whom having not seen, ye love; in whom, though now ye see him not, yet believing, ye rejoice with joy unspeakable and full of glory" (I Pet. 1:8).

John wrote, "That which we have seen and heard declare we unto you, that ye also may have fellowship with us: and truly our fellowship is with the Father, and with his Son Jesus Christ. And these things write we unto you, that your joy may be full" (I John 1:3,4). Peace that passes understanding and abundant joy is the everlasting heritage of the child of God. Jesus purchased that joy for us on Calvary's tree.

Because of Calvary

Because of Calvary today I have found peace,
A peace long sought in worldly paths of sin;
A peace that slipped elusive through enchanted ways,
And vanished ere I gained an entrance in.

Because of Calvary today I have found joy,
A joy that will not tarnish nor grow dim;
A joy that will not perish with the using,
But constant, radiant, glows as some bright gem.

Because of Calvary today I have found hope,
A blessed hope that brightens all my way;
A hope to which I cling steadfast, secure
That I shall see my Lord some glorious day.

Because of Calvary! Because of Calvary!
May this thought shape my life beyond today,
That He who died eternal life to give
Is now to me the Life, the Truth, the Way.

Because of Calvary, O Lord, no longer I delay:
Because of all Thy love has done for me
Today I yield my life, my love, my all,
Thine evermore, because of Calvary.

Yes, we are debtors because of the peace, the joy, the
hope, the way, the truth, and the life we have because of
Calvary.

Salvation From Hell

We are debtors because Christ has delivered us from
Hell. But for the matchless grace and shed blood of Jesus
Christ we would be destined to spend eternity in Hell. Think
of that—Hell, with its privation—no water, no food, no
sleep, no rest! Hell with its godlessness—no churches, no
Christian homes, no Christians, no Bible, no Christ, no
Holy Spirit, no Heavenly Father! Hell with its ugliness—
no blushing flowers, no grassy slopes, no waving fields of
grain, no dewy vales, no nodding trees, no babbling brooks,
no running streams, no cooling breezes, no beauty of any
kind. Hell with its promiscuous mob—"the fearful, and unbelieving, and the abominable, and murderers, and whoremongers, and sorcerers, and idolators, and all liars" (Rev.

21:8). Hell with all of its woe—the cursing, and weeping, and wailing, and gnashing of teeth, the burning of the fires of perverted passion, the burning of the fires of guilty consciences, the burning of the fires of sulphur and brimstone in God's eternal penitentiary.

Christian, Jesus Christ has saved us from all of that and more! We are under infinite obligation. We are debtors because of all of this and Heaven, too. We have "an inheritance incorruptible, and undefiled, and that fadeth not away, reserved in heaven for you."

> Go wing your flight from star to star—
> From world to luminous world;
> As far as the universe spreads its wall.
> Take all the joys of all the spheres
> Multiply each through endless years—
> One minute of Heaven is worth them all.

Paul considered himself a debtor because God had deigned to save his soul.

II. SPECIAL REVELATION

Secondly, Paul considered himself a debtor because of a special revelation God had given him. Paul was an apostle. He tells us in the first verse of Romans that he was called to be an apostle. One qualification of an apostle was that he had seen Jesus in Person and had received his commission from the very lips of the Saviour. Paul was converted on the Damascus road. There he met Jesus face to face. Later, he tells us, he was caught up into the third Heaven and saw Jesus in Person and saw things it was not lawful for him to utter.

Jesus said of Paul to Ananias, the prophet in Damascus, "Go thy way: for he is a chosen vessel unto me, to bear my name before the Gentiles, and kings, and the children of Israel" (Acts 9:15). Having this high calling and the commission of an apostle, Paul felt keenly his responsibility.

While we are not apostles we have received the New Testament through the apostles and the Old Testament through
the prophets. We have the verbally inspired, infallible,
authoritative, eternal, and blessed Word of God. *We have
the Truth!* "Sweeter also than honey and the honeycomb,"
"More to be desired...than gold."

Quest for Truth

The sages and the philosophers of the ages have sought
for truth. Diogenes hunted it with a lantern. Intellectuals
have looked for it with the flickering torch of reason. The
blind have led the blind into pitfalls and chasms of despair,
death, destruction, and everlasting doom!

Philo of Alexandria probably climbed higher up the tower
of philosophy than any non-Christian who ever reasoned.
He combined the best of Greek philosophy with the philosophy of Judaism and wrote of a mediating, divine Logos, a
divine logic, or reason, or Word emanating from God, but
he never came to the fact, so profound and yet so simple
that, "In the beginning was the Word, and the Word was with
God, and the Word was God" (John 1:1). He never reached
the truth that "the Word was God" nor that "the Word was
made flesh, and dwelt [tabernacled] among us, (and we beheld his glory, the glory as of the only begotten of the Father,) full of grace and truth" (John 1:14).

We Have the Truth

My friends, we have the Truth and with that Truth we
have incumbent upon us the responsibility to tell it forth.
We are debtors! "Ye shall be witnesses unto me both in
Jerusalem, and in all Judaea, and in Samaria, and unto the
uttermost part of the earth" (Acts 1:8).

> We've a story to tell to the nations
> That shall turn their hearts to the right,
> A story of truth and mercy,
> A story of peace and light.

We've a song to be sung to the nations
That shall lift their hearts to the Lord,
A song that shall conquer evil
And shatter the spear and sword.

We've a message to give to the nations
That the Lord who reigneth above
Hath sent us His Son to save us,
And show us that God is love.

We've a Saviour to show to the nations
Who the path of sorrow hath trod,
That all of the world's great peoples
Might come to the truth of God.
                                    —Colin Sterne

Power of God

Paul said, "I am a debtor both to the Greeks, and to the Barbarians; both to the wise, and to the unwise. So, as much as in me is, I am ready to preach the gospel to you that are at Rome also. For I am not ashamed of the gospel of Christ: for it is the power of God unto salvation to every one that believeth; to the Jew first, and also to the Greek" (Rom. 1:14-16).

Paul had seen the Gospel of Christ work among the Jews at Antioch and in the synagogues on Cyprus, and in Pamphylia, and in Pisidia, and Galatia. He had seen it work also with the sophisticated Greeks in those places and in Ephesus and Troas and Macedonia, and Athens and throughout all of Greece. He had confidence that this glorious message which was "to them that perish foolishness; but unto us which are saved...the power of God" (I Cor. 1:18) would work in Rome also, the seat of political power and imperialism.

God's Word Not Bound

And when he finally got to Rome and was in prison there

he wrote the church at Philippi and said, "But I would ye should understand, brethren, that the things which happened unto me have fallen out rather unto the furtherance of the gospel" (Phil. 1:12). And in his final imprisonment in Rome in that dark, cold, granite Mamertine prison where he was held until he was taken out and beheaded, he wrote Timothy, "Remember that Jesus Christ of the seed of David was raised from the dead according to my gospel: Wherein I suffer trouble, as an evildoer, even unto bonds; but the word of God is not bound" (II Tim. 2:8,9).

III. APOSTLESHIP

Paul felt also that he was a debtor because of his apostleship which we have referred to. Not only does the fact that we, too, have Paul's message obligate us but we also have a commission from God. Every Christian is to "do the work of an evangelist." In Romans 1:6 the apostle says, "Among whom are ye also the called of Jesus Christ." In the following verse he says, "called to be saints." In Ephesians 4:11, 12 he tells us that Christ has given "some, apostles; and some, prophets; and some, evangelists; and some, pastors and teachers; For the perfecting of the saints, for the work of the ministry."

Christians Called

A young man asked me if I thought he had been called to the ministry. I answered, "If you are a Christian you are already in the ministry. You may be recreant to your responsibility but you are in the ministry. I do not mean that God has necessarily called you to be an ordained minister or that He has called you to stand in the pulpit and preach but every Christian is called as a witness and is called to serve."

Full-Time Ministry

Some are called to a full-time ministry, some as evangelists, some as pastors, some as teachers, some as missionaries. How wonderful it is to be called to the full-time ministry! I would not take all the money in the world for my call to preach. I fought the call when first it came, but within a few days I surrendered and I have been proclaiming this glorious Gospel for more than thirty-five years.

A Privilege to Preach

What a privilege! "How beautiful upon the mountains are the feet of him that bringeth good tidings, that publisheth peace; that bringeth good tidings of good, that publisheth salvation" (Isa. 52:7). I respect people in nearly all pursuits of life, merchants, farmers, doctors, mechanics, day laborers, lawyers, governors, senators, presidents, and kings, but I envy not one of them. I had rather be an old-time preacher of the old-time Gospel that has warmed this cold world's heart for two thousand years than to be the President of the United States! Angels would be glad to have my job!

I am a stranger here, within a foreign land.
My home is far away upon a golden strand,
Ambassador to be of realms beyond the sea,
I'm here on business for my King.

This is the message that I bring,
A message angels fain would sing:
"O be ye reconciled,"
Thus saith my God and King,
"O be ye reconciled to God."

This is the King's command,
That all men everywhere
Repent and turn away
From sin's seductive snare;
That all who will obey
With Him shall reign for aye,
And that's my business for my King.

My home is brighter far than
Sharon's rosy plain,
Eternal life and joy throughout its vast domain.
My Sov'reign bids me tell
How mortals there may dwell,
And that's my business for my King.

IV. NEED OF ALL

Fourthly, Paul regarded himself a debtor because of the need among all nations. In verse 13 he says, "Now I would not have you ignorant, brethren, that oftentimes I purposed to come unto you, (but was let hitherto,) that I might have some fruit among you also, even as among other Gentiles" (Rom. 1:13). What deep sympathy Paul demonstrates for people he had never seen! In his concern he reflects the passion of Jesus. Jesus is touched with anything that touches us. Stone a member of His body and He cries, "Why persecutest thou me?" "Inasmuch as ye did it not to one of the least of these, ye did it not to me" (Matt. 25:45). Here we see the deep, passionate sympathy of Jesus. Paul asked, "Who is weak, and I am not weak?" Here we see the deep, passionate sympathy of Paul.

You may sit down at a piano and strike a note. If you hold open that note and strike the same note one octave higher the note that is held open will respond. The entire keyboard of Paul's soul was open. He responded to the cries and sighs of his fellowmen everywhere. A man all the way across the Aegean Sea cried, "Come over into Macedonia, and help us," and a corresponding note in Paul's soul began to vibrate, "Come over into Macedonia, and help us!" They are not all recorded, but he was hearing cries every day— pain-filled, fear-filled voices, calling out in the night, voices from Corinth, from Athens, from Rome, and from distant Spain.

"From jungles far away, from town and hamlet small
Come cries from souls sin-bound and doomed to endless woe."

Wherever there was a need it found response in the heart of Paul. He wrote to the Galatians, "My little children, of whom I travail in birth again until Christ be formed in you" (Gal. 4:19). He wrote to the Philippians, "For God is my record, how greatly I long after you all in the bowels of Jesus Christ" (Phil. 1:8). He wrote to the Colossians, "For I would that ye knew what great conflict I have for you, and for them of Laodicea, and for as many as have not seen my face in the flesh" (Col. 2:1).

Christian, does the cry of the world's needs find an open note in your heart? Or are the strings of your soul so muffled by the cares of this life they no longer respond to the cries of lost and dying men? Oh, my friends, this world is steeped in darkness and sin and so little is being done to carry out the Great Commission.

Consider the Need

Consider the spiritual needs of this world! Half the people who have ever lived since the creation of man are living now! There are 340,000 births and only 165,000 deaths every day. This means that there is a net increase of 175,000 people every day—a net increase of more than 63 million every year. Only about one in thirty of this increase are being reached personally with the Gospel each year.

Godless, Christ-hating communism now dominates one billion people. American communists spend 38% of their income for the spread of their nefarious doctrine. American Christians spend less than one cent per individual per day for foreign missions.

Money Spent

According to statistics released by the Christian and

Missionary Alliance this is how Americans spend some of their money each year:

Food	$81,140,000,000
Housing	59,461,000,000
Household Operation	57,980,000,000
Cars and Transportation	51,555,000,000
Clothing, Accessories, Jewelry	40,018,000,000
Medical Care	25,211,000,000
Recreation	23,824,000,000
Alcoholic Drinks	11,100,000,000
Tobacco	8,100,000,000
Personal Care	6,778,000,000
Religion and Welfare	5,791,000,000
Pets	3,500,000,000
Dog Food and Care	210,000,000
Foreign Missions	192,000,000

There are approximately three million villages in the world without a resident gospel witness. More than half the people in the world do not know the way of salvation. The Bible still waits to be translated into more than 1500 languages and dialects. At the present rate of progress this would take at least 150 years!

Who Cares?

David cried, "No man cared for my soul!" Do you not care for the souls of men? A missionary who had come home with broken health pleaded to go back to the field. He was asked why he wanted to return. He answered, "Because I can't sleep for thinking of them!" Most Christians cannot think of them because they are so inclined to sleep. You sit before the television set and sip a cup of coffee or a glass of cola and watch the newscast, a veritable cup full of horrors. And as you watch it does not add a single tang to your refreshment. Oh, careless, prayerless, passionless Christian, how can you be so hard?

The Dead and the Dying

You hear the report of the dead and the wounded on the battlefield. You hear of three armed robberies in the area and realize that in a thousand other cities the same thing is going on. You view the debris and carnage of drunken driving and hear the report that 50,000 Americans are slain annually on the nation's highways. Then your program is interrupted for a beer ad and drinking is glorified. You hear of the divorce of a prominent person, and of embezzlement by a public official. Then you get impatient for the weather report and the sportscast. The dark record of the day never haunts the night with the mingled wails of the bereaved and the damned! How can you heal the wounds you do not feel? How can careless hearts ever be effective heralds of the passion of Jesus?

The Lost World

Oh, my friend, this old world is lost! "The whole world lieth in wickedness" (I John 5:19). In this city there is a home—no, a house where live a man and wife with a good income. They have every material thing that it seems a normal couple would want—but there is no happiness in that home. The old demon, Rum, resides there with them. They started taking little social drinks, they formed the habit, then they began to drink constantly until they realized that they were in the awful grip of that devastating habit. They have tried to quit but are powerless to do so. They need Jesus!

Lost Man

Over there is a man whose health is wasting away. He has an incessant cough and the doctors tell him he has emphysema, his lungs are leathery and his breath often must be taken in gasps. Cigarettes have nearly killed him and the doctors tell him that if he does not quit smoking he will soon die. Chain smoker that he is, he has been able to quit for short periods but always goes back to his cigarettes after a few hours. He needs the Saviour.

Lost Girl

Yonder is a girl who has sacrificed the most precious possession she had, her virtue for popularity. She never intended to go that far and after it happened she wept and told herself it would never happen again. But temptation came and she fell again. And now it has been constant and her life is ruined. What can she do? Who can help her? Did not Someone give living water to a sinful woman at a well one day? Did He not cast demons out of Mary Magdalene? Who can help this girl? Why, Jesus can, of course!

Lost Boy

There is a boy who followed the crowd and became a thief and there is the crowd he followed and they are thieves, too. They are in the grip of sin and are holding each other there. Who can deliver them? Jesus can set them free and 'if the Son shall set them free they shall be free indeed.'

> I know of a world that is sunk in shame,
> Of hearts that faint and tire.
> I know of a name, a name, a name
> That can set that world on fire!

And can make every drunkard sober and can make every harlot pure and every thief to steal no more! His name? We call His name Jesus.

The World Condemned

The world is under the judgment of God. "Now is the judgment of this world: now shall the prince of this world be cast out" (John 12:31). Jesus came not "to condemn the world, but that the world through him might be saved" (John 3:17). The world was condemned before Jesus came. It was condemned when the subtle serpent ceased to walk uprightly and was made to crawl upon his belly in the dust of the ground. It was condemned when the first man committed his first sin. "He that believeth on him [Jesus] is not condemned: but he that believeth not is condemned already, because he hath not believed in the name of the only begotten Son of God" (John 3:18). Yes, the world is now under condemnation.

Christ Will Save

The world is in a crisis today.
The powers of Hell are set in stern array.
Men are blind and cannot find the way.
Christ, our Lord, will help us in our plight.
Christ for the Crisis! He is the Source of Light.

The solution is not to fix conditions but to fix men! This does not mean that we pay no attention to conditions or that we do not try to better conditions, also. It means that while we may work at relieving symptoms of the disease of sin, the real solution is to get at the cause of the symptoms.

Ready to Preach

Paul was ready to preach the Gospel at Rome. He was not ashamed of that Gospel for it was "the power of God unto salvation to every one that believeth; to the Jew first, and also to the Greek."

Do you believe, my friend? If you do, tell the good news to others! If you do not, come and trust the Saviour now.

IV

A Prayer of Divine Passion

"Then said Jesus, Father, forgive them; for they know not what they do."—Luke 23:34.

I hesitate to touch the picture of the Saviour on Calvary's cross lest I leave my fingerprints upon it. Yet there is no other scene in all eternity, historical or prophetical, which will so convict and convert and call and consecrate as that picture of the Son of God on the cross.

Behold Him

See Him there between two thieves with the bloodthirsty mob around laughing, mocking, jeering, sneering, reviling, cursing, and challenging Him to come down. Human hatred had reached its climax. The Lord of Glory hanged with hands and feet nailed to a cross of wood, brow torn with thorns, face beaten to a swollen mass, back lashed to purple shreds, tongue dry from the sting of vinegar and bitter from the taste of gall, lips cut with cruel fists and exposed to the burning sun, and ears dulled by the ceaseless cries of the rabble: "Away with Him!" "Crucify Him!" "Impostor!" "We have no king but Caesar!" "Deceiver!" "Hail, King of the Jews!" "If thou art the Son of God, save Thyself!" "Come down from the cross and we will believe that Thou art the Son of God!"

He Could Have Come Down

Jesus could have come down from the cross. He could have stepped down off that cross just as He stepped from His heavenly throne down to the manger of Bethlehem. But if He had done so they would have said, "He performed a miracle. He pulled Himself off the cross," but they would have denied His deity. He did not accept the challenge to come down to prove that He was God. He stayed on the cross and proved it. He proved it by dying, and then rising from the dead. He is "declared to be the Son of God with power...by the resurrection from the dead" (Rom. 1:4).

"Then"

"Then said Jesus, Father, forgive them; for they know not what they do." "Then" when every nerve was strained to the utmost and became a path for the sharp, hot feet of pain to walk upon; "then" as they heaped their scorn upon Him, as they hurled their satire in His teeth; "then" when they deserved to have the earth swallow them as it swallowed Korah and his confederates; "then" when He could have spoken and more than twelve legions of angels would have come to His rescue—"then" He prayed.

Held by His Passion

Now, He could have come down from the cross, but there is a sense in which He could not have come down. He had become sin for us. Since "He saved others" He could not save Himself. His passion held Him fast to a cross of wood. It was the Father's will and not the spikes of steel which held Him there. He was nailed to the cross. They had placed the cross on the ground and stretched Him upon it, the rough wood pressing into his lascerated and bleeding back. His hands were stretched out and a nail was driven through each of them into the wood. The cross was then raised and dropped into its socket with a flesh-tearing thud so that the weight of His body pulled against two nails. This was to expand the chest cavity making it difficult to breathe and to hasten death. His feet were then pulled up on the upright of the cross as far as they could lift them and one spike served to hold them both driven through into the wood.

Difficult to Speak

The entire weight of His body pulled against three nails so that the prophecy of Psalm 22:14 was fulfilled: "I am poured out like water, and all my bones are out of joint." If the Father's will were to be done He must drink the bitter cup of sacrificial sufferings to the dregs and thus it was not "possible that this cup" should "pass from" Him. His strength was "dried up like a potsherd" (Ps. 22:15).

Hands and Feet Nailed Fast

He could no longer lift up His hands to bless, to touch lepers and make them clean and take dead children by their hands and cause them to live. His hands were nailed fast to the cross. He could no longer walk the dusty roads of Galilee and the limestone cliffs of old Judea. His feet were spiked to the wood. He could no longer teach and preach in the Temple and in the synagogues and on the mountainsides.

He Could Pray

But there was something He could do. He could pray. So He prayed. He did not wait until He got on the cross to pray. He spent whole nights in prayer. He taught us that "men ought always to pray, and not to faint" (Luke 18:1). He prayed without ceasing and even when He came to die He prayed this earnest prayer out of compassion for His crucifiers.

When He Could Do Nothing Else

"Then"—when He could do nothing else He prayed. By praying this prayer "then" Jesus taught us that we can always pray. There are no trials so great that you cannot serve God in the ministry of prayer. I talked with a sweet old lady in a charity rest home. For over two years she had lain flat on her back, her hands trembling with palsy and her body racked with pain. She said, "I am ready to go on to be with the Lord. My days of usefulness are gone.

There is nothing I can do now except to pray. I pray for you. I pray for the missionaries and I pray for many others." That old saint is serving God. Her days of usefulness were not over when she was confined to a rest home. God answers prayer.

In Great Pain

It was in great pain that Jesus prayed. Nailed as He was to the cross with the cavity of His chest expanded it was necessary for Him to pull up on those nails to get enough breath to pray. The tense of the Greek word used here would indicate that He kept on saying, "Father, forgive them; for they know not what they do."

Jesus' Prayer Answered

"Then said Jesus, Father, forgive them; for they know not what they do." Do not imagine that those words were simply an expression which fell from the lips of Jesus just to show us that He was willing to die. They show us that He was willing to die, but they have far greater significance. They were no mere expression. They were a prayer that rang from the depth of His soul and reached the ear of the Father. Fifty days later on the day of Pentecost 3,000, and on the following day 5,000 of those who knew not what they did were converted. Jesus had prayed, "Father, forgive them; for they know not what they do." Peter said, "I wot that through ignorance ye did it." Why were 8,000 people converted in two days' time? It was not simply because the Holy Spirit came at Pentecost, although without His presence they would not have been saved. They were not converted simply because of Peter's eloquence, although he preached eloquently and boldly the blessed Gospel as he was filled with the Holy Ghost. But a multitude was converted in answer to Jesus' prayer.

"Father, Forgive Them"

Now, notice that Jesus did not take His prerogative as God

to forgive them. He was as much God as was the Father, but He was a man. He was just as human as if He had not been God. He was the unique God-Man. When Jesus was born of the virgin He did not cease to be God. He did not lay aside the qualities of deity, but He laid aside the independent exercise of those qualities. He did not lay aside the exercise of His divine qualities, but the *independent* exercise of those qualities. He became dependent upon God the Father and God the Holy Spirit.

He Obeyed the Father

His very motto was, "I come to do thy will, O God." He said, "My meat is to do the will of him that sent me" (John 4:34). In Gethsemane He prayed, "Not as I will, but as thou wilt." In order that Jesus might be a perfect human being, subject to human limitations and that He might stay in character as a man yet never cease to be the infinite God, He turned the reigns of His life over to God the Father and God the Holy Spirit. He was led by the Spirit into the wilderness to be tempted of the Devil. He performed all of His miracles in the power of the Holy Spirit. When at the first miracle in Cana of Galilee, when as Milton wrote, "Conscious water knew its Lord and blushed," it was the Holy Spirit who changed the water to wine. When at the grave at Bethany Jesus cried, "Lazarus, come forth!" it was the Holy Spirit who quickened the decaying flesh of the sleeping Lazarus. When on the Sea of Galilee Jesus said to the wind, "Cease blowing!" and to the waves, "Be still!" it was the Holy Spirit who changed the stormy sea to a limpid, starlit mirror and wrought that holy hush.

As a Man He Prayed

Jesus was God, but He was a man. As a man He prayed, "Father, forgive them," and in so doing He taught us to pray. If the prayer of Jesus was answered, our prayers will be answered. Jesus based His plea upon His own merit, and we must base our plea upon His merit, too, and not upon our own. Then God will answer our prayers as certainly as He answered Jesus' prayer.

A young lady came to me one day and said, "Dr. Parker, I want you to pray for me. I know God will answer your prayer."

I answered, "I will be glad to pray for you, but you know God will answer your prayers as certainly as He will answer mine."

She said, "But my prayers do not seem to go any higher than the ceiling."

I said, "So what? God is not confined to a realm above the ceiling. We pray, 'Our Father which art in heaven.' It is literally 'Our Father who art in the heavens.' He is in the third Heaven and in the stellar heaven, and He is also in the atmospheric heaven. He is here and He is accessible to you. If my prayers are answered, they are answered not because I am good, but because of Jesus' righteousness. On the other hand, I cannot pray a genuine prayer if I regard iniquity in my heart."

If Jesus' signature is honored at the bank of Heaven when the check is made out to "cash," it will be honored when the check is made out to you or me.

Forgiveness Needed

"Then said Jesus, Father, *forgive* them; for they know not what they do." The one thing for which He prayed for them in His dying hours was forgiveness. That was their primary need. They did not know what they were doing, but they needed forgiveness. They ought to have known what they were doing. Ignorance is not innocence. "And this is the condemnation, that light is come into the world, and men loved darkness rather than light, because their deeds were evil" (John 3:19). Jesus taught that they needed forgiveness despite their ignorance and spiritual darkness. They, of course, knew that they were putting to death an innocent

Man and that He claimed to be God. They knew that they
were wrong for they had shut out any conviction of the truth,
but they did not know the enormity of their crime. My
friend, if you are without the Lord Jesus Christ, you know
that you are a sinner but you do not realize the depth and
loathsomeness of your sins. Someone has said that these
people knew what they were doing, but that they did not know
what they were doing. They did not know the extent of their
offense. Oh, how blind the sinner is! Why would anyone
reject the Saviour? Why do men live in sin? Surely they do
not know what they are doing.

No Hard Cases

"Then said Jesus, Father, forgive *them*." Who were they?
They were a mixed multitude, a heterogeneous mob. There
were evil characters from the underworld, curious dere-
licts of humanity who had simply followed the crowd to see
the excitement, hardened soldiers of Rome who could gam-
ble at the foot of His cross for the garments of a dying
Christ, and old, long-bearded Pharisees, steeped in religious prejudice and pride, self-righteous, religious people, the hardest people on earth to reach for God. Yes, all
of these and others were there. His disciples were there.
His mother was there. And, my friends, you and I were
there represented in that crowd. We were included in His
prayer because our sins were upon Him and helped to crucify Him. But notice that He did not make exceptions. He
did not regard the salvation of any a thing too hard for God.
Say, there are no hard cases with God. If you know the
most wretched sinner on earth, you find him and tell him
that Jesus can save him. If you have sunk to the very depth
of sin and degradation you need not despair. Jesus loves
you and included you in His prayer.

Forgive

The connotation of the word "forgive" used by Jesus on

this occasion not only included the idea of expunging their sins but it was also a plea for the Father to hold back the judgment they deserved. I can imagine more than 144,000 (twelve legions) of angels poised in the heavens waiting to sweep the rabble into Hell. But Jesus cries, "No, Father, please do not destroy them. Don't pour out Your fury upon them. Pour it upon Me. Forgive them!"

> I stand amazed in the presence
> Of Jesus the Nazarene,
> And wonder how He could love me,
> A sinner, condemned, unclean.
>
> How marvelous! how wonderful!
> And my song shall ever be:
> How marvelous! how wonderful
> Is my Saviour's love for me!

Why I Am a Christian

The thing that brought me to Christ is a realization that Jesus loved me. I say it to my shame: I had been a church member more than ten years but had never been saved. I was eighteen years of age and was a devotee of worldly pleasure. My godly parents were so concerned about me that I voluntarily went to Sunday school one day just to make them feel better about me. I had often gone, but always because my parents insisted on it. But on this particular Sunday the superintendent asked me if I would teach a class. I protested that I was not fit to teach a class but he insisted that I was. I took the class, but I did not want to be a hypocrite, so I said, "If I am going to teach Sunday school I will have to live a Christian life, so I will cut out my sins."

Good Resolutions

I resolved to quit drinking. I was not a drunkard. I could take a drink or leave it alone. The fellow who can do that usually takes it. I decided to quit gambling. I did not play the roulette wheels, but I used to bet on the ball games. It is as certainly gambling to match for a Coca-Cola as it is to shoot craps in a dirty back alley. It is as surely gambling to take a chance on an automobile which is being raffled off by some apostate church as it is to play poker in a greasy, back room in some pool hall. Gambling is gambling whether it is done by society people at the bridge table or gambling professionals in Las Vegas.

Religious but Lost

I resolved to quit cursing. Now, I never formed the habit of taking God's name in vain. I do not deserve any credit for that, but when I was a little child I heard an old man say, "If you could breathe your own air to take God's name in vain it might not be so bad; but when you use the air that God gives you to keep you alive to curse His holy name, that is the height of ingratitude." I always had a contempt for an ingrate and I did not want to be one so I was careful not to form the habit of profaning the name of God. But my language was not clean because "out of the abundance of the heart the mouth speaketh." My heart was not clean so my words condemned me. I catalogued my sins and resolved to quit them. I resolved to serve God and be faithful in religious duties, but I was not saved. I kept my resolutions very well but I could not live the Christian life because I did not have the Christian life. Salvation is a Person and that Person is Jesus. Someone has said, "Trying to be a Christian without Christ is like trying to pump water out of a dry well." That is what I was trying to do.

I Needed Jesus

On Sunday morning as I tried to teach the Sunday school lesson it dawned on me that what I needed was Jesus. The lesson was on "The Martyrdom of Stephen." When Stephen had been stoned by the angry mob and was dying he saw Jesus "standing on the right hand of God" and "he kneeled down, and cried with a loud voice, Lord, lay not this sin to their charge" (Acts 7:55,60). There was a reference to the Saviour's prayer, "Father, forgive them; for they know not what they do." When I read this to my Sunday school class I said, "Boys, you see, Stephen had the spirit of Christ. He prayed for those who put him to death. Jesus prayed for those who crucified Him. And you know, our sins nailed Jesus to the cross." When I said that I realized for the first time in all my life the truth of it. Then I said, "Boys, I am a sinner. I have never been saved. I am not fit to teach your class. But right now I will trust Christ as my Saviour." I bowed my head and wept and so did the boys. That moment I was born again. I am a Christian because the realization of the mighty love of Christ gripped my soul. My friend, He loves you, too. Will you trust Him now?

V.

Looking for a City

"We have an altar, whereof they have no right to eat which serve the tabernacle. For the bodies of those beasts, whose blood is brought into the sanctuary by the high priest for sin, are burned without the camp. Wherefore Jesus also, that he might sanctify the people with his own blood, suffered without the gate. Let us go forth therefore unto him without the camp, bearing his reproach. For here have we no continuing city, but we seek one to come."—Heb. 13:10-14.

The Bible Dramatic

The Bible is the most dramatic book ever written. God has illustrated spiritual truth with thousands of practical experiences, objects, materials and relationships.

As the children of Israel wandered in the wilderness with their lowing, bleating, bawling, dusty, diseased and dying herds and flocks of cattle, sheep and goats, there was tremendous need for laws of sanitation and laws governing the preservation and the butchering of the cattle. God gave these laws to Moses in the Levitical system.

The Law Practical and Typical

The law of Moses consisted of "commandments" expressing the righteous will of God, "judgments" governing the civic life of the people, and "ordinances" governing the religious life of the people. The ordinances as well as the judgments were intensely practical and both contained great spiritual truths.

The Day of Atonement

On the Day of Atonement the high priest would bring three animals to the altar, a bullock and two lambs. These were lambs of the goats. We would call them kids. The bullock was sacrificed for the sins of the high priest. One of the lambs was reserved to be used as a scapegoat and the other lamb was sacrificed for the sins of the people. After the high priest went into the sanctuary, the holy of holies, and sprinkled the blood of these animals in the presence of the manifested glory of God he came out of the sanctuary and turned the bodies of those animals over to another priest. This priest took those bodies out into the wilderness and burned them. The law did not allow the priests to eat of them as it allowed them to eat of many of the daily sacrifices. There was a place out in the wilderness outside of the camp known as "the place of ashes" where the "bodies of those beasts" were burned. God instituted those Old Testament ceremonies. He knew that Jesus would be crucified outside the gate. "Wherefore Jesus also, that he might sanctify the people with his own blood, suffered without the gate" (vs. 12).

Jesus an Outcast

I say it reverently, but Jesus Christ is an outcast of human society. "He was in the world, and the world was made by him, and the world knew him not" (John 1:10). Jesus made the world. I do not mean the material universe. He made that, too, but He made the world of men, the *kosmos*, the organized world system. He established human government. But when He came into the world which He made the world knew Him not. "He came unto his own, and his own received him not" (John 1:11). That is, He came unto His own things. The word "own" is in the neuter gender. It has reference to things. "And his own received him not." Here the word "own" is in the masculine gender and therefore has reference to people. He came unto His own things, His own realm, His own kingdom, but His own people received Him not. They said, "Away with him, away with him, crucify him." They said, "We have no king but

Caesar." They said, "His blood be on us, and on our children."

Jesus went to Jerusalem to be rejected and crucified. "And Jesus going up to Jerusalem took the twelve disciples apart in the way, and said unto them, Behold, we go up to Jerusalem; and the Son of man shall be betrayed unto the chief priests and unto the scribes, and they shall condemn him to death" (Matt. 20:17,18). This prophecy was fulfilled. Jesus was rejected and if He should come back today and preach the same doctrine He preached two thousand years ago He would be rejected again if He showed promise of becoming King. Let Him stand up in this materialistic age and say, "If any man will come after me, let him deny himself, and take up his cross, and follow me." Then let Him make a triumphal entry toward a throne and He would again be crucified. We do not use that means of capital punishment today but if we did He would find Himself outside the city hanging in purple shreds on a cross. Let Him come back and say, "Blessed are the pure in heart: for they shall see God." This sin-loving, pleasure-mad generation would cry, "We will not have this man to reign over us." This world is against Jesus. There were many who waved palm branches and strewed flowers in Jesus' pathway and cried, "Hosannah to the Son of David," who eight days later joined the rabble crying, "Crucify Him! We will not have this man to reign over us!"

The World Against Jesus

This world is against Jesus Christ. Do not kid yourself about it! He said, "My kingdom is not of this world: if my kingdom were of this world, then would my servants fight, that I should not be delivered to the Jews: but now is my kingdom not from hence" (John 18:36). The world is against Jesus and if you belong to Jesus the world is against you. "We know that we have passed from death unto life, because we love the brethren" (I John 3:14). If it is a ground of as-

surance that one is saved because he loves the brethren, if
he is not saved he does not love the brethren. Oh, you may
love your brother in the flesh or you may love your wife in
a human way though you are not saved, but you do not love
him or her in the spiritual sense. You do not love them as
Christians. Somebody says, "If I trust Christ as my Saviour I will have to give up my friends." Oh, no you won't!
You take a clear-cut stand for Jesus Christ and they will
give you up!

A Gulf Fixed

There is a line drawn separating Jesus from this world.
He was crucified "without the gate." There is a gulf fixed
with the world on one side and Jesus on the other. You cannot be on both sides. Jesus said, "He that is not with me is
against me; and he that gathereth not with me scattereth
abroad" (Matt. 12:30).

John wrote, "Love not the world, neither the things that
are in the world. If any man love the world, the love of the
Father is not in him" (I John 2:15).

James wrote, "Whosoever therefore will be a friend of the
world is the enemy of God" (Jas. 4:4). Of course, we are
to love the souls of men and we are to love the world in the
sense that God loved when "he gave his only begotten Son,
that whosoever believeth in him should not perish, but have
everlasting life." But we are not to love the vainglory of
this godless age. The "friendship of the world is enmity
with God" (Jas. 4:4).

Now Jesus is without the gate and we are called to "go
forth" unto Him without the camp. That is where we are to
stand spiritually. Geographically we are in the world, but
as Jesus stated in His high priestly prayer in the seven-
teenth chapter of John, we are in the world but we are not of
the world.

Our Relevance to the World

Now as long as we are in the world we have a responsibility here. We are to "render unto Caesar the things that are Caesar's," and we are to let our 'light so shine before men, that they may see our good works, and glorify our Father which is in heaven.' Like the apostle, "I am a debtor ...both to the wise, and to the unwise." It has always been true that the church of Jesus Christ is "the salt of the earth." But if the salt loses its savor it is good for nothing but a sidewalk. The salt in Russia lost its savor and the Marxists walked all over it. The salt in Germany lost its savor and Hitler and his Third Reich goose-stepped all over it. It has lost its savor in other nations and has been cast out and walked upon. And if we do not have a turning back to God through the Lord Jesus Christ, wicked men will walk over the American church and turn it into the handmaiden of the state! I am not preaching the so-called social gospel, but the social aspect of the Gospel of salvation through our Lord Jesus Christ.

Why Jesus Came

Jesus did not come into the world to condemn the world. The world was condemned before He came. It was condemned when Adam and Eve ate the forbidden fruit. It was condemned the moment God said, "Cursed is the ground for thy sake" on the day when the subtle serpent ceased to walk uprightly and was made to crawl on his belly in the dust of the earth. The world was already condemned. Jesus came that "the world through him might be saved. He that believeth on him is not condemned: but he that believeth not is condemned already, because he hath not believed in the name of the only begotten Son of God" (John 3:17,18).

Christ Outside

Now Christ is without the camp. The world cast Him out. They hanged Him on a cross. We must go out and 'bear His reproach' or we must line up against Him. "No man can serve two masters: for either he will hate the one, and love the other; or else he will hold to the one, and despise the other. Ye cannot serve God and mammon" (Matt. 6:24).

Must Bear Reproach

The text makes it clear that if we go outside the camp to stand with Jesus we must bear reproach. I do not like reproach. I have no martyr complex. It is not because it is my nature to choose reproach and shame and ridicule that I go out to Jesus. It is not because I like crosses and dying groans, and darkness, and suffering, and the place of a skull that I go without the camp to bear reproach. It is because Jesus is an outcast and if we stand with Him it must be without the gate.

The World Is Attractive

It is not because the world can have no appeal for me that I am a consecrated Christian. It is not because I have no carnal nature.

> This old world we live in
> Is mighty hard to beat.
> We get a thorn with every rose
> But ain't the roses sweet?

This is a wonderful world with its mighty ships plowing the deep, with its planes jet-propelled, with its radio and television and atomic power, with its superstructure of nations, with its majestic cities rearing their skyscrapers into the blue, with its power politics and commerce and challenge.

Victory Through Christ

I will confess to you that the world makes a strong bid for me. I have not got rid of my carnal nature. I reckon myself "dead to sin" but there are propensities that remind me that the carnal nature is present. The Word of God has taught me that I must "keep under my body," but the old nature is there. The apostle cried, "Who shall deliver me from the body of this death?" Then he thought of the only One who has power to deliver. He who delivered us from the penalty of sin and one day will deliver us from the presence of sin can also deliver us from the power of sin. The apostle must have pressed down hard on the parchment as he wrote, "I thank God through Jesus Christ our Lord. So then with the mind I myself serve the law of God; but with the flesh the law of sin" (Romans 7:25). Victory comes through rising above the flesh in the power of the risen Christ. It comes through positive fellowship with Jesus Christ.

There Is a Hell

It is not simply because there is a Hell that I am saved. There is an eternal lake of fire in which all Christ-rejecters will suffer forevermore. "But the fearful, and unbelieving, and the abominable, and murderers, and whoremongers, and sorcerers, and idolaters, and all liars, shall have their part in the lake which burneth with fire and brimstone: which is the second death" (Rev. 21:8). I do not want to go to Hell. That fact helped get me under conviction but did not bring me to Jesus.

There Is a Heaven

It is not simply that there is a Heaven that I am saved. There is a wonderful place called Heaven. Jesus said, "In my Father's house are many mansions: if it were not so, I would have told you. I go to prepare a place for you. And if I go and prepare a place for you, I will come again, and receive you unto myself; that where I am, there ye may be also" (John 14:2,3). We learn from this that in God's house there is a place prepared for Christians. It is a beautiful place, glorious beyond the conception of our finite minds! It

took God only six days to make this world, array it with
blushing flowers, nodding trees, dewy vales, grassy slopes,
and running streams, and crown it all with His masterpiece
—man. Jesus Christ left this world almost two thousand
years ago. He said, "I go to prepare a place for you." If
He has spent one one-thousandth of that time preparing
Heaven for us, what a wonderful place it must be! I would
not miss going there for all the world, but that is not the
main reason I am saved.

Joy in Christ

It is not primarily because of the satisfaction, the peace,
the happiness and the abundant joy that is found in Christ
that I am saved. Happiness is not found outside of Jesus
Christ. There is real joy in fellowship with Jesus Christ.
John wrote, "And these things write we unto you, that your
joy may be full" (I John 1:4).

The Christian Life Is Practical

The Christian life is not simply a practical life; it is *the*
practical life. It is not practical to be without Christ. Since
God can look into the future ten, twenty, thirty or forty
years from now, and since He is able to make "all things
work together for good to them that love God," the only
practical life is the God-planned, God-directed life. But
this is not the main reason I am a Christian.

Why I Am a Christian

I am a Christian because it dawned on me one day that Jesus loved me, a sinner, unworthy and condemned, deserving nothing better than Hell and deserving Hell. This love
got hold of me. It drew me to Jesus.

> Beneath the cross of Jesus
> I fain would take my stand,
> The shadow of a mighty Rock
> Within a weary land;

A home within the wilderness,
A rest upon the way,
From the burning of the noontide heat,
And the burden of the day.

Upon that cross of Jesus
Mine eye at times can see
The very dying form of One
Who suffered there for me;
And from my smitten heart with tears
Two wonders I confess—
The wonders of His glorious love
And my own worthlessness.

I take, O cross, thy shadow
For my abiding place;
I ask no other sunshine than
The sunshine of His face;
Content to let the world go by
To know no gain nor loss,
My sinful self my only shame,
My glory all the cross.

Outside the Camp

Jesus is outside the camp. He was crucified outside the gate—outside the gate of a city, the gate of a nation, and the gate of the world.

The World Hates Jesus

The world hates Jesus—Jesus, who filled Heaven with glory in eternity past—Jesus whom angels and seraphs and cherubs adore—Jesus, the Creator who upscooped the valleys and upreared the mountains and covered them all with light—Jesus, the Babe of Bethlehem, whom simple shepherds and humble wisemen sought—Jesus, the Nazarene, who sweat great drops of blood and bore a shameful cross—Jesus, the Son of God, who conquered Death and Hell. The world hates Jesus.

Jesus Loves the World

Jesus loves the world—that poor, lost, wicked world, confounded at Babel, out of which He called the ancient Abram—that world which lieth in the arms of the wicked one—that cruel world which gave Him a manger for a cradle, thorns for a crown, a cross for a throne, and a bitter sponge for a king's cup. Jesus loved the world. Oh, the matchless love of Jesus!

> I stand amazed in the presence
> Of Jesus, the Nazarene,
> And wonder how He could love me,
> A sinner, condemned, unclean.

Make Your Choice

Choose between the city and Calvary. That is what a Scots lad and a Scots lassie did. A young Scotsman was called home from college at the death of a very godly older brother. Self-righteous but lost he requested to be in the room alone for awhile with his brother's corpse. There in the room he faced his need of Jesus Christ and accepted Him as Saviour and Lord. When he returned to college he told his sweetheart what he had done. In the crisis this brought to her she chose the world and rejected the Saviour and broke her engagement to the young man who was destined to be the great Scots preacher, Robert Murray McCheyne. When his sweetheart told him her decision he wrote:

> She has chosen the world and its paltry crowd!
> She has chosen the world and its endless shroud!
> She has chosen the world and its misnamed pleasures!
> She has chosen the world before Heaven's own treasures!
>
> She has launched her boat on life's giddy sea!
> And her all is afloat for eternity.
> But Bethlehem's star is not in her view
> And her aim is far from the harbor true.

When the storm descends from the angry sky,
Ah! Where from the winds shall the vessel fly?
Away, then—oh, fly from the joys of earth!
Her smile is a lie—there's a sting in her mirth!

When stars are concealed and rudder gone,
And Heaven is sealed to the wandering one,
The whirlpool opes for the gallant prize;
And with all of her hopes to the deep she flies.

But who may tell of the place of woe,
Where the wicked dwell, where the worldlings go?
For the human heart cannot conceive
What joys are the part of them who believe.

Nor can justly think of the cup of death
Which all must drink who despise the faith.
Come! Leave the dreams of this transient night,
And bask in the beams of an endless light.

Take Your Stand

Now you must take your stand outside with Jesus or inside against Jesus. Outside the gate are reproach and
crosses and dying groans and sorrow and darkness. Inside the gate of the city are light and laughter and music
and fun and achievement and honor and a sparkling cup of
pleasure. Young people, do not let anybody tell you that
there is no fun in sin. There is a lot of fun in sin. Every
draught from the cup of pleasure gives a thrill. The cup
sparkles and scintillates and shines. Take your stand and
let us see what we have.

Choosing the City

Do you choose the city? Let us see what you have. Laughter? I heard laughter but it was the hollow, harsh guffaw of
a godless world. There was no music in it. And now me-
thinks that instead of laughter I hear the screaming wails of

the damned. There was music. But it was the cheap, off-beat, syncopated jazz of a godless world. There is in every draught from the cup of pleasure a thrill. But every draught contains a bit of poison. And in the bottom of the cup are twisted dregs and in the dregs is a scorpion with the sting of death. For the cup that thrills is a cup that kills.

There is light. Yes, but it is a cheap, artificial, garish, neon light with no radiance—and now it flickers and goes out. Now there is darkness as black as Hell's sable badge and pitchy scowl. There are skyscrapers but now in the lightning flash of God's awful judgment I see in their stead yawning atomic craters. "For here we have no continuing city."

One day New York, builded on a veritable rock, will sink into its famous harbor. London, the queen city of the earth, will fall. Quaint, beautiful San Francisco will tumble into rubble. Rome, "the eternal city," will sink into eternal night. Tokyo and Paris and Berlin and Moscow and Madrid and Los Angeles and Chicago will pass away. "For here we have no continuing city."

Jerusalem Fell

Just six years after our text was written Jerusalem was destroyed. A million Jews were in Jerusalem for a special event. Titus came with the Roman legions and surrounded the city. For forty days the people were shut up in the city of Jerusalem without supplies from without. Women literally ate their babies behind the walls of Jerusalem. Finally Titus put a battering ram against the wall and broke it down. They entered the city and razed it. Not one stone was left upon another in the Temple, as Christ had predicted.

Outside the Camp

When we stand outside the camp with Jesus, what do we have? These are not dying groans; they are shouts of victory! This is no place of death but a place of life. This is not a cross. As I bore it, it was a cross but the touch of God has turned it to a throne! This is no tomb. It is a gate of pearl! This is not Golgotha. This is a pearly white city with foundations of jewels whose Builder and Maker is God!

The City to Come

"For here we have no continuing city, but seek one to come." We seek one coming. It is sure to come.

"And I John saw the holy city, new Jerusalem, coming down from God out of heaven, prepared as a bride adorned for her husband.... And the building of the wall of it was of jasper: and the city was pure gold, like unto clear glass. And the foundations of the wall of the city were garnished with all manner of precious stones.... And the twelve gates were twelve pearls; every several gate was of one pearl: and the street of the city was pure gold, as it were transparent glass. And I saw no temple therein: for the Lord God Almighty and the Lamb are the temple of it. And the city had no need of the sun, neither of the moon, to shine in it: for the glory of God did lighten it, and the Lamb is the light thereof."—Rev. 21:2, 18, 19, 21-23.

Who Is Outside?

Who will be without the gate then? Not the child of God! We will be with Jesus inside the city, the pearly white city, the city foursquare, the city of God! "For without are dogs, and sorcerers, and whoremongers, and murderers, and idolaters, and whosoever loveth and maketh a lie" (Rev. 22:15). "And there shall in no wise enter into it any thing that defileth, neither whatsoever worketh abomination, or maketh a lie: but they which are written in the Lamb's book of life" (Rev. 21:27).

Sinner, if you will trust Jesus, your name will be written in that book. Trust Him now! He will save you!

VI

Death Takes No Holiday

I invite your attention to two portions of Scripture. The first one is taken from Hebrews 9:27. *"It is appointed unto men once to die, but after this the judgment."* The second is a portion of Psalm 82:7. *"Ye shall die like men."*

Multiplied millions of human beings have fallen before the "grim reaper." Talmage called death "a wicked king" whose "palace is a sepulchre, his pleasure fountains the tears of a weeping world and his flowers the faded garlands on coffin lids." The rider of the pale horse never takes a holiday!

A Melancholy Fact

Poets have wreathed the brow of Death with flowers, but his head is more ghastly because of his floral diadem. For the bereaved death is a sad fact. Even the Christian Alfred Lord Tennyson wrote:

> Break, break, break
> On thy cold grey stones, O sea!
> And I would that my tongue could utter
> The thoughts that arise in me.
>
> O well for the fisherman's boy,
> That he shouts with his sister at play.
> O well for the sailor lad,
> That he sings in his boat on the bay!
>
> And the stately ships go sailing on
> To their haven under the hill;
> But, oh, for the touch of a vanished hand
> And the sound of a voice that is still!

Break, break, break
At the foot of thy crags, O sea!
But the tender grace of a day that is dead
Will never come back to me.

A Universal Fact

Death is a melancholy fact and it is also a universal fact.
Only two of the race have escaped and they escaped because
God would illustrate the coming rapture of the church and if
you escape it will be because of the soon coming of the Lord
Jesus Christ and the fact that you have been born again by
faith in Him. But if Jesus tarries, "Ye shall die like men."
Noah escaped the flood in an ark and it is written, "Noah
lived after the flood three hundred and fifty years. And all
the days of Noah were nine hundred and fifty years: *and he
died"* (Gen. 9:28,29). Shem, Ham and Japheth died, and
Abraham died, and Isaac died, and Jacob died, and Joseph
died, and Pharaoh died, and there arose another Pharaoh
who knew not Joseph and he died and all the firstborn of
Egypt died and the history of the world has been the history
of Death. Death never ceases his work. He takes no holiday!

Great Men Die

Nebuchadnezzar, the Chaldean, built the Golden City and
welded the little Babylonian kingdom into a mighty empire,
BUT HE DIED and left it. Cyrus, the Persian, conquered
Babylon, BUT HE DIED. Alexander the Great conquered
Egypt and Persia and Asia and sat down in Babylon at the
age of twenty-four and wept because there were no more
worlds to conquer, BUT HE DIED in the welter of a drunken
debauch.

Death lays his icy hands on the great men of the earth as
well as upon the weak and ignominious. He touches the king
who must lay aside his scepter and lie down beneath the sod
like the beggar. He puts his cold finger on the doctor who

must write his last prescription, lie down and die. The driver must leave his truck on the highway, his cargo un-delivered, and give his brawny and stalwart frame to the embalmer's knife. The carpenter must put down his ham-mer and saw and change his coveralls for a shroud. The mother must kiss her helpless babes good-by and leave them. The innocent child must drop his toys and grapple with the iron strength of the monster Death for "in Adam all die" (I Cor. 15:22).

A Terrible Calamity

Not only is death a melancholy and a universal fact, but it is also a terrible calamity to the sinner. It is a calamity to the sinner in the first place because memory to the dying man is very strong. To the sinner in his dying hour mem-ories are not "precious memories"; they are anything but precious. Like a flash of lightning memory brings before the dying sinner the panorama of his entire life. He re-members the days of his childhood, the many solemn warn-ings that came to him, the prayers of godly parents, the peeling of the chimes in the tower ringing out the strains of an old familiar hymn, the testimony of a friend, the earnest exhortation of the family pastor, and many experiences call-ing him to Jesus. Then dark memories like "unclean and hateful birds" begin to gather and perch above his bed. There they sit and croak. The memory of profanity, blas-phemy, obscenity, theft, desecration of holy things, lust, adultery, pride, moral cowardice, lying, and many other black ravens of memory stick their beaks into the con-science of the dying man.

Good-by to Pleasure

Death is a terrible calamity to the sinner because he must say good-by to all of his pleasures. The drunkard must leave his liquor, but not his craving for it. The rich man in Hell cried out for a drop of water. He had no water to drink for he had to leave all his comforts, but his appetite was still with him.

The adulterer and the adulteress will have to leave their paramours. The gambler must leave his gambling table, his cards, his dice, his wheels of chance and all of his ill-gotten gain. The worldling will have to say good-by to his dancing and petting. He will leave his cigarettes and cock-tails. His pleasures will all be over and he must go to a land of misery and woe.

Come on, rich man! Count your money! Compute your assets! What is the value of your stock? How much are your bonds worth? Appraise your real estate! Figure the cash value of your insurance! Check your cash! Count it all! Pile up your wealth and gaze upon it, for you will never see it again.

Come on, great man! Senator, judge, governor, general! Say a long farewell to all your greatness, for now you go to a land of contempt and agony and misery and woe! Mr. President, look out for the assassin's bullet!

Death Ends Opportunities

In the next place, death is an awful calamity to the sinner because it closes the door of opportunity for him to be saved. It is too late for the sinner to be saved after death. You may not live another day after you receive this warning.

Death Is Imminent

Death is imminent. It is liable to come at any moment. In a southern city I talked with a woman who said she was too busy to attend church. Within two hours after our con-versation she was killed by a speeding automobile as she left her place of business. In the same city I talked with a man about his soul who promised me that he would give the matter serious consideration. The following Sunday evening he refused to attend services with his mother and his daugh-ter saying that if he went to church he would have to make a decision. During the church service that night a man walked into his house and cut his throat, severing the jugular vein, and he died without regaining consciousness.

Calamity of the Judgment

Death is a terrible calamity to the sinner because "it is appointed unto men once to die, but after this the judgment." What a dreadful experience that will be! Sinner, one day you are going to stand before Jesus Christ. He will turn His soul-searching eyes into your heart and ask for an accounting. What will you say to Jesus? You can give me excuses, but you will stand dumb in the presence of the Great Judge of all the earth.

> "He is there! He is there
> To judge the world,"
> Aloud the archangel cries;
> And thunders roll from pole to pole,
> And lightning cleaves the skies.

What will you say when He begins to read your sins? Will you give the flimsy excuse that you were too busy for God? Will you claim that you thought that the Holy Bible was a hoax and that God was a liar? Will you blame the hypocrite in the church? Will you try to tell Jesus how good and righteous you are? No! You will stand dumbfounded, not only stripped of reasons, but also stripped of excuses. You will stand there trembling and weeping convulsively until the sentence is passed and you hear the words, "Depart from me, ye cursed, into everlasting fire!" All around men, women and children weep and wail and scream and curse, and gnash their teeth. But they are not weeping for you. Some may turn their wrath upon you because of the godless influence you had upon them. Some may weep for you.

Parents will weep over their lost sons and daughters and especially over the fact that they are lost because they themselves were lost. They are miserable in their own condition and doubly wretched because of the lost condition of those whom they influenced in the godless course. The rich man in Hell did not want his five brothers to come to Hell.

I dreamed that the great judgment morning
Had dawned, and the trumpet had blown;
I dreamed that the nations had gathered
To judgment before the white throne;
From the throne came a bright shining angel
And stood on the land and the sea,
And swore with his hand raised to Heaven,
That time was no longer to be.

And oh, what a weeping and wailing,
As the lost were told of their fate;
They cried for the rocks and the mountains,
They prayed, but their prayer was too late!

The Wailing of the Wicked

On one occasion when the Lord rebuked the children of Israel "the people lifted up their voices, and wept. And they called the name of that place Bochim" (Judges 2:4,5). Bochim means "weepers." The people on that occasion wept in repentance and got right with God. It was a time of great weeping. At the judgment of the wicked dead it will be too late for repentance, but the mightiest volume of weeping in the history of the world will reverberate in space. The thunder of the cries of the damned will resound to other planets and the angels will remember the judgment of the wicked as a mighty Bochim.

The Second Death

Death to the sinner is a terrible calamity, because beyond the grave and beyond the judgment is the second death.

"There is a death whose pang outlasts this fleeting breath.
O what eternal horrors hang around one's second death!"

"But the fearful, and unbelieving, and the abominable, and murderers, and whoremongers, and sorcerers, and idolators, and all liars, shall have their part in the lake which burneth with fire and brimstone: which is the second death."—Rev. 21:8.

Two Pictures

When Princess Elizabeth Petrovna became heiress to the throne of Russia she almost decided to decline to reign. One of her counsellors, Lestocq, however, came to her with two paintings. Both were of the princess, one of her in a dismal prison cell and the other of her on the throne wearing the imperial crown. After looking at the two paintings, without hesitation she chose the crown.

If I could give you a Bible picture of Hell with all of its contempt and misery and agony and remorse, and another picture of Heaven with its love and bliss and comfort and peace, I believe you would immediately decide to flee the wrath to come, accept Jesus Christ as your personal Saviour and become an heir of life eternal.

Punishment of the Wicked

We find something about the punishment of the wicked on nearly every page of the Word of God. In the third chapter of the Bible we find that God placed a curse upon the serpent, the woman, the man, and even the ground because of sin. The many arguments against an eternal Hell spring from a common source. That fountainhead is the claim that God is too good to allow man to suffer eternal damnation in Hell.

The Love and Wrath of God

God is good. He is infinite in His goodness. He is also infinite in His wrath. His capacity for love and goodness requires a capacity for hate and wrath. "God is love," yet He pronounced a curse upon man. If He will curse man, He will damn man. If He will damn man, He will damn man for all eternity. God allowed little innocent Japanese babies to suffer in Hiroshima and Nagasaki. If He will let innocent people suffer in this life, why do you think He will not let guilty people suffer in the life to come?

No tongue could tell the depth of wretchedness contained in the inspired sentence which fell from the lips of Love Incarnate when He said, "These shall go away into everlasting punishment" (Matt. 25:46).

Hades and Hell

"Hell" is the word generally and unfortunately used to translate the Hebrew word *Sheol* in the Old Testament and the Greek word *Hades* in the New Testament. These words refer to the place where all disembodied spirits went before Jesus Christ arose from the dead and where the spirits of the lost go now. Before the resurrection of Christ it was divided into two parts—the abode of the blessed and the abode of the damned.

Paradise and Tartarus

Jesus told us that the rich man 'lifted up his eyes in hell' (Hades). He was in the abode of the damned. When he saw the beggar in Abraham's bosom, he was looking into Paradise, the abode of the blessed. When Jesus was on the cross He said to the thief, "To day shalt thou be with me in paradise" (Luke 23:43). In His sermon on the day of Pentecost Simon Peter quoted from the Sixteenth Psalm, "Thou wilt not leave my soul in hell" (Acts 2:27) and said that it had reference to Christ. "He seeing this before spake of the resurrection of Christ, that his soul was not left in hell [Hades], neither his flesh did see corruption" (Acts 2:31).

Before the resurrection of Christ all the believers who died went to Sheol, that is Hades, into the compartment called "Paradise." The unsaved went into the compartment where the rich man was.

Sins Covered

Sins were not taken away until Jesus died. They were covered but not expiated. When Jesus shed His blood on the cross the sins were actually forgiven, and when He arose He led "captivity captive." He carried all the redeemed of the Old Testament home to Heaven with Him. Now when a believer dies he goes straight to Heaven to dwell with God and the angels and the saints of the ages, but when a sinner dies he goes to Hades.

Lake of Fire

At the end of the ages when Jesus sits upon the great white throne, the lake of fire (or what we think of as the actual Hell) will be opened. "And the devil that deceived them was cast into the lake of fire and brimstone...and shall be tormented day and night for ever and ever" (Rev. 20:10).

"And the sea gave up the dead which were in it; and death and hell [or Hades] delivered up the dead which were in them: and they were judged every man according to their works. And death and hell were cast into the lake of fire. This is the second death" (Rev. 20:13,14). Oh, the eternal horrors of Hell!

A Place of Joy

But just as sure as there is a place of eternal torment for the Christ-rejecter, there is a place of eternal joy for the Christian. It is a beautiful place, glorious beyond the conception of our finite minds. It is a comfortable place. There is no pain there.

Jesus Is There

Yes, it is a city of pure gold, with jewel foundations, jasper walls, pearly gates, and crystal fountains, where there is no pain, but more wonderful than that, thank God, it is where Jesus is!

"...where I am, there ye may be also." That makes it Heaven—the presence of Jesus Christ. We will know each other there. We will mix and mingle and cross each other's path forevermore, but Jesus Christ makes it Heaven. Jesus Christ is the Light thereof. 'Oh, the land of the cloudless day!'

What are the foolish pleasures of this world compared with the eternal joys of Heaven? Turn your back on sin, and the life that leads to Hell, and accept Jesus Christ as your personal Saviour. You have no lease on life. "It is appointed unto men once to die."

Death of the Christian

To the Christian death is no calamity. It is just going Home. It is just the passing through the river into the land of eternal joy. One time an old Christian was dying. His son stood by his bed and asked, "Father, how does it look down in the valley?"

The old man asked, "What valley do you mean?"

The boy answered, "The doctor says you are in the valley of the shadow of death."

"Oh," said the old man, "the doctor doesn't know what he is talking about. There are no shadows about this bed. I am in no valley. I am on a sunlit summit."

"Precious in the sight of the Lord is the death of his saints."—Ps. 116:15.

I stood by my mother's dying bed in a hospital in Selma, Alabama. She had lain unconscious for hours. Flowers had been brought into the room but she had not seen them. Suddenly she opened her eyes and said, "There are so many of them."

I said, "So many what, Mother?"

She answered, "So many flowers."

I said, "Yes, there are a lot of flowers."

She said, "Aren't they beautiful?" Then she said, "And there are so many angels."

I said, "Yes, Mother, there are a lot of angels."

Then she said, "Aren't the walls beautiful?"

I looked at the old grey hospital walls and I did not see anything very beautiful about them but I knew she was looking at walls I could not see—jasper walls—and I said, "Yes, Mother, the walls are beautiful." She fell asleep and woke up on the other side of those jasper walls.

A Great Man of God

It was my privilege to know the great radio preacher, Paul Rader. Years ago in Florida I went with him and other friends to the beach for a swim in the Gulf of Mexico. Dr. Rader showed me a trick he knew and lifted me bodily above his head. He was a man of tremendous physical prowess. In fact, when he was in seminary he was a pugilist fighting under an assumed name. He did better than he anticipated. He was in line to box for the heavyweight championship of the world. Lest he be discovered as a pugilist and a ministerial student, he quit the ring. Later he quit the ministry because he had never been saved. He became a college football coach and finally went into some kind of "wildcat" oil well business. They struck it rich so he wired his wife, "We are fixed." She wired back, "Fixed for what?" He began to wonder what he was fixed for. He went to his hotel room and read his Bible for two days and nights until he found Christ as his Saviour. Then he went down and preached on the street. Later he pastored the Moody Church for two years. He served as president of the Christian and Missionary Alliance and built the great tabernacle in Chicago.

When Paul Rader died he weighed less than 100 pounds. Merrill Dunlop, who worked with him, stood by his bedside and wept. Mr. Rader asked him, "Who is dying around here, Merrill? Why are you crying? I am not dying. I died twenty-seven years ago when I trusted Christ. Let's not cry. Let's sing." Later, when Mr. Dunlop had gone, Mr.

Rader woke up from a nap and asked Mrs. Rader if Merrill cried any more. Then he said, "Tell Merrill I am not dying. Tell him I died—." Mrs. Rader said, "Twenty-seven years ago?" He nodded his head and fell asleep in Jesus.

Jesus Experienced Death

Death to the man who is right with God is not a woe. "Ye shall die like men." But Jesus Christ has pulled the sting out of Death for those who trust in Him! The mighty Conqueror, the Lord Jesus Christ, has vanquished Death. "But we see Jesus, who was made a little lower than the angels for the suffering of death, crowned with glory and honour; that he by the grace of God should taste death for every man" (Heb. 2:9). The Greek word translated "taste" contains the thought of taste in the sense of experience. It does not necessarily carry the idea of just a taste but has the connotation of entering into an experience. In other words, "Jesus experienced death for every man." He voluntarily submitted Himself to man's great enemy, Death.

Jesus said, "Therefore doth my Father love me, because I lay down my life, that I might take it again. No man taketh it from me, but I lay it down of myself. I have power to lay it down, and I have power to take it again" (John 10:17,18).

Jesus' Death a Miracle

It was a miracle that Jesus could die. Death is the result of sin and Jesus was without sin. He was not subject to "the law of sin and death." Only the blood of Jesus Christ could loose us from our sins. It was necessary for Him to die if we should be saved so 'He gave Himself.' In that short sentence Jesus is both the Object and the Subject. He was given but He did the giving. That wonderful thought got hold of me and I tried to find a song that would express it. When I could find none I wrote the following.

> When Christ, my Lord, atonement made
> Himself upon the cross He laid.

High Priest of God, yet Lamb was He,
Whose blood was shed to set me free.
And now He sits at the Father's side
That all who trust may be justified.

The Lamb of God, who gave His life,
Yet Priest of God, who drove the knife,
A Lamb hanged on the cross to bleed,
A Priest, whose blood our cause did plead.
And now He sits at the Father's side
That all who trust may be justified.

Tempted like men, yet standing true,
Hating your sin, yet loving you.
Touched by your infirmity,
He lives to plead through eternity.
Even now He sits at the Father's side
That all who trust may be justified.

Christ a Captive

Jesus conquered Death. He allowed Himself to be taken
captive by that "wicked king." He went with that awful enemy of mankind into the murky caverns of Death's dark domain. There He allowed Himself to be bound with the
shackles of Death. He lay down for three days in a rock-
hewn, air-tight cave with a huge stone fitted snugly into the
mouth of it. His head and body were wrapped in graveclothes cemented with a hundred and fifty pounds of spike-
nard. Jesus was dead. He lay cold and stiff in death. The
cruel monarch on the throne clapped his bony hands and
hoarsely shrieked sepulchral cries of victory.

Weeping friends and disciples slowly left the horrible
scene of man's greatest crime at Golgotha and went back to
the city—grief-stricken and dejected. Frightened centuri-
ons and rulers drank and reveled in debauchery and tried
to forget the dreadful scene which they will never be able to
forget unless they turned in faith and repentance to the Sav-

iour whom they crucified. Cowardly scribes and fearful priests retreated to their council rooms to devise a scheme to keep Jesus in the tomb. The great stone in the mouth of Joseph's tomb could be sealed by the authority of Rome and a garrison could be placed at the grave. This they did in a vain effort to keep Christ the Captive of King Death.

Jesus lay dead for three days. But when three days passed He stirred. He broke the chains that bound Him. He reached up on the throne and pulled down the "wicked king" and cast him to the dank floor of the dungeon. The crown rolled off the head of Death. Then Jesus put His heel on the neck of Death and pulled out his sting, picked up the fallen crown and put it on His own head, took the keys of Death, broke the cerements of the grave and walked out a risen, living, victorious Saviour.

> Low in the grave He lay—
> Jesus my Saviour!
> Waiting the coming day—
> Jesus my Lord!
>
> Vainly they watched His bed—
> Jesus my Saviour!
> Vainly they seal the dead—
> Jesus my Lord!
>
> Death cannot keep his prey—
> Jesus my Saviour!
> He tore the bars away—
> Jesus my Lord!
>
> Up from the grave He arose,
> With a mighty triumph o'er His foes;
> He arose a Victor from the dark domain,
> And He lives forever with His saints to reign.
> He arose! He arose! Hallelujah! Christ arose!

Sinner, come to this wonderful, life-giving Saviour! He

"tasted death" for you in order that He might present you with everlasting life. Jesus said, "I am the resurrection, and the life: he that believeth in me, though he were dead, yet shall he live: And whosoever liveth and believeth in me shall never die" (John 11:25, 26). Believe in Him now!

> Come, every soul by sin oppressed,
> There's mercy with the Lord,
> And He will surely give you rest
> By trusting in His word.
>
> Only trust Him, only trust Him,
> Only trust Him now;
> He will save you, He will save you,
> He will save you now.

VII

Choose Your God

I would like for you to turn with me to Joshua, chapter 24, and follow as I read the first fifteen verses.

"And Joshua gathered all the tribes of Israel to Shechem, and called for the elders of Israel, and for their heads, and for their judges, and for their officers; and they presented themselves before God. And Joshua said unto all the people, Thus saith the Lord God of Israel, Your fathers dwelt on the other side of the flood [this word ought to be translated "river." It is the word *nahar* which means a great flow of water. Here it has reference to the river Euphrates where Abraham and his fathers dwelt. I call attention to this because it has relevance to the message I shall bring.]..."

"Your fathers dwelt on the other side of the river in old time, even Terah, the father of Abraham, and the father of Nachor: and they served other gods. And I took your father Abraham from the other side of the flood [river], *and led him throughout all the land of Canaan, and multiplied his seed, and gave him Isaac. And I gave unto Isaac Jacob and Esau: and I gave unto Esau mount Seir, to possess it; but Jacob and his children went down into Egypt. I sent Moses also and Aaron, and I plagued Egypt, according to that which I did among them: and afterward I brought you out. And I brought your fathers out of Egypt: and ye came unto the sea; and the Egyptians pursued after your fathers with chariots and horsemen unto the Red Sea. And when they cried unto the Lord, he put darkness between you and the Egyptians, and brought the sea upon them, and covered them; and your eyes have seen what I have done in Egypt: and ye dwelt in the wilderness a long season.*

"And I brought you into the land of the Amorites, which dwelt on the other side of Jordan; and they fought with you: and I gave them into your hand, that ye might possess their

land; and I destroyed them from before you. Then Balak the son of Zippor, king of Moab, arose and warred against Israel, and sent and called Balaam the son of Beor to curse you: But I would not hearken unto Balaam; therefore he blessed you still: so I delivered you out of his hand. And ye went over Jordan, and came unto Jericho: and the men of Jericho fought against you, the Amorites and the Perezzites, and the Canaanites, and the Hittites, and the Girgashites, the Hivites, and the Jebusites; and I delivered them into your hand. And I sent the hornet before you, which drave them out from before you, even the two kings of the Amorites; but not with thy sword, nor with thy bow. And I have given you a land for which ye did not labour, and cities which ye built not, and ye dwell in them; of the vineyards and oliveyards which ye planted not do ye eat. Now therefore fear the Lord, and serve him in sincerity and in truth: and put away the gods which your fathers served on the other side of the flood [river], *and in Egypt; and serve ye the Lord. And if it seem evil unto you to serve the Lord, choose you this day whom ye will serve; whether the gods which your fathers served that were on the other side of the flood* [river], *or the gods of the Amorites, in whose land ye dwell: but as for me and my house, we will serve the Lord."—Josh. 24:1-15.*

If the people decided not to worship Jehovah, the true God of Heaven, then they must choose some other god or some other gods. Everybody has a god or gods of some kind. In ancient times every city and every pursuit of life had its particular god or goddess.

Athena

Athens was the city of Minerva, the goddess of wisdom. Her Greek name was Athena. The city was named for her. Standing on Mars' Hill where Paul preached the sophisticated Greeks under conviction you can look across to the nearby Acropolis and see the Parthenon, the most famous building in the world. It has stood for more than twenty-five hundred years, the marvel of architecture. In this famous building the Greeks worshiped the goddess of wisdom. Millions of people bow down at the shrine of their own intellect and worship this goddess who, though she may not be seen in marble statue, is as cold and lifeless today as she was sitting, gold-embossed, in a cold marble chair on that cold marble hill in Athens twenty-four centuries ago.

Diana

Ephesus was the city of the goddess of the chase, the goddess of the hunt. She has her devotees today in those who place their very souls on the altar of sports. Good, clean sports are wholesome and beneficial if not overindulged and worshiped. In their fanatical devotion to Diana the Ephesians were stirred to a frenzy against Paul and his companions. At the bottom of the situation was the lust for money on the part of those who sold the copper images of the goddess. In America sports have been so commercialized that they have lost much of their benefits as the wholesome part of our educational system which they ought to play.

Venus

In ancient days female vanity bowed down to Venus, the goddess of love, so-called. It was an inordinate love. Eros, the Greeks called this kind of love. Venus was the personification of lasciviousness. There are millions who worship at her shrine. They feast their eyes upon the nudity and moral looseness of the stage and screen and exult in that which is lewd and vulgar.

Bacchus

There was the ancient god Bacchus. I have seen his ruined temples in many places. At Baalbek, once known as Kieropolis, the City of the Sun, where the sun-god was the chief deity, there is a complex of ruined temples. One was the temple of Zeus, or Jupiter, the sun-god. One was the temple of Venus. The most impressive was the temple of

Bacchus. Here are granite columns approximately eight feet in diameter, sixty feet in length and reared one upon another. Some are still standing; others are lying on the ground. These huge columns are so heavy there is not a crane on earth that would lift one of them. You could not get enough men close enough to it to lift it. And yet, the ancient Romans had them hewn from the Aswan quarries in upper Egypt, floated hundreds of miles down the Nile, across the Mediterranean, brought them over the Lebanon range, up near the border of Syria between the Lebanon and the Anti-Lebanons and in some ingenious way built into temples. There is, in this massive temple where the people worshiped, the god of wine.

Fanaticism

That god has his temple in nearly every community on earth. See the temple with great columns of human skulls with dry, ghastly eyeholes, with bloody altars upon which men, women and children sacrifice all that is good and noble and precious! See that man sacrifice his reputation and his character! See that woman sacrifice her beauty and her virtue! See that man and wife sacrifice their lovely children! See that youth sacrifice the hearts of loved ones! See that man sacrifice his wealth, and that one his home! See them sacrifice their very souls!

When I see what whiskey does for people—how it caused one man to crash across a highway and kill a loved one of mine; how it caused another to take his own life, and another to kill his wife (for I stood at a prison cell and talked with a man sentenced for killing his wife. He said to me, "I did not kill her. Liquor did it!" I had to answer, "But you drank the liquor")—I say, when I see what liquor does for people I think Shakespeare must have been almost inspired when one of his characters said that men "put an enemy in their mouths to steal away their brains."

Some Kind of God

Everybody has some kind of a god. I remember years ago when dear old Dr. Huston, a great fundamental, evangelistic, Southern Baptist was pastor of the First Baptist Church of Miami, Florida. I went down there to hold an evangelistic campaign. On the way down when we stopped in Jacksonville a lady sat down by me and asked if I were a tourist. It seemed to startle her when I told her that I was an evangelist. She asked me where I was from. In those days I was on the administrative staff of Bob Jones University. I told her this. She said, "I have heard of Bob Jones University. That is a reactionary school, isn't it?" I answered, "Yes, if you mean that it is against communism, modernism, atheism, agnosticism, and all so-called scientific adulterations of the Gospel. But, no, if you mean that it is negative in its approach." The woman began to talk very loudly as if she wanted to be heard by all of the other passengers. I do not like a loud private conversation but I began to talk loudly, too, because if she were going to attack my cause before all those passengers I had to defend it.

She said, "I did not know that educated people believed in God any more."

I said, "All the scholarship is not on the side of the Devil. The greatest scholars I have ever known believe the Bible from cover to cover."

She said, "Incidentally, I received my M. A. from a certain university and I received my Ph.D. from another university in New York City. And all the people who got their doctorates when I got mine were atheists."

I said, "That is too bad, but you know everybody has some kind of a god."

She said, "I will grant that there is a universal religious instinct. You will find people in all parts of the world worshiping their several gods. But some of us have outgrown the antiquated idea of a god."

I said, "Lady, you have some kind of a god."
She said, "No, I do not have any kind of a god."
I said, "Yes, you do."
She said, "No, I do not."
We were still talking out loudly.
I said, "I think I can tell you what your god is."
She answered. "All right. What is my god?"
I said, "I think it is a Ph.D. from a certain university."
A good old Christian woman sitting behind us said, "Amen!"

Ideal

Everybody has some kind of a god. You may worship at the shrine of your own puny intellect, or you may worship at the shrine of your own passions. But you have some kind of an ideal. Your ideal is your idol. The word "idol" connotes the thought of ideal. Your ideal is your idol. If Christ is not your God, you have a false ideal. You are guilty of idolatry. Now, Joshua said, "If it seem evil unto you to serve the Lord [Jehovah], choose you this day whom ye will serve." In other words, "If you decide against serving the true God of Heaven, then choose from the other gods which one you are going to serve, for everyone serves some kind of a god."

Alternatives

Joshua mentioned three alternatives. If they decided not to serve the true God they could serve the gods which their fathers had worshiped on the other side of the river Euphrates, or the gods of the Egyptians, or the gods of the Amorites in whose land they dwelt.

Gods of the Mesopotamians

What could those gods do for Israel? What could the gods their fathers worshiped beyond the Euphrates in Chaldea and in Mesopotamia do for those who worshiped them? Those gods were the so-called teraphim, the little household gods such as those Rachel stole from her father Laban and hid in the camel's furniture and sat upon while her father searched the camp of Jacob. Connected with the worship of the teraphim was the superstitious idea that these little inanimate icons could protect the household from harm and danger. Some of our superstitious friends have little images of St. Christopher and St. Joseph on the dashboards of their cars and believe these little dolls when blessed by a priest can protect them from wrecks. I saw one on the dashboard of a car with the front end bashed in. I saw a big league pitcher pull one out of his baseball shirt and cross himself with it. He put it back, wound up and threw the ball to big Hank Greenberg. Hank knocked the ball over the fence!

Abraham Called Out

What had those little teraphim done for their fathers? Had not Jehovah, the God of Heaven, called Abraham out of Ur of the Chaldees and out of Mesopotamia, and brought him into the Land of Promise? Joshua recounts the history of his people to show the superiority of Jehovah to the gods of the heathen.

Gods of Egypt

What could the gods of Egypt do for the Egyptians? The Egyptians worshiped the sun and they worshiped cattle. They also worshiped the many creatures such as Jehovah used to plague their land—frogs, lice, flies, and locusts. What could these things do for them? Had not Jehovah made bare His mighty arm and delivered Israel from Egyptian bondage, while Egypt was plagued and the firstborn in every Egyptian home died, and Pharaoh's army drowned in the Red Sea?

Exodus in Brief

Moses set forth the Book of Exodus in brief in Deuteronomy 4:34: "Or hath God assayed to go and take him a nation from the midst of another nation, by temptations, by signs, and by wonders, and by war, and by a mighty hand, and by a stretched out arm, and by great terrors, according to all that the Lord your God did for you in Egypt before your eyes?"

Gods of the Amorites

What could the gods of the Amorites do for their devotees? Jehovah had driven out the two kings of the Amorites. He had sent the hornets before Israel and had driven out the people from their homes and Israel now possessed their villages. Joshua spoke of the "gods of the Amorites" but the Hivites, and the Hittites, and the Girgashites, and the Canaanites worshiped the same gods. The tribes of Amor were more numerous and were dominant. Also, they were among the first peoples of the Promised Land Israel encountered, so Joshua referred to "the gods of the Amorites."

I used to read of Israel's conquest of Canaan and wondered how a God of love and a God of justice could destroy even the innocent babies and how He could command Israel to take that land. Then one day I heard Dr. Bob Jones, Sr., say that he wondered about that. But he said he did not have all the facts. He said he learned that those people were diseased. If God had not destroyed them they would have contaminated the entire human race. Then he said, "It is not an unkind thing to kill a cow to save a herd." When I was studying archeology in New York City I asked the professor, an eminent archeologist, about this. To answer my question he gave a series of lectures. When he was finished I had concluded that if God had not wiped out these old Canaanitish civilizations to at least the extent to which He did that indeed they would have contaminated many other peoples.

One day I was reading the Book of Genesis and I read that God said unto Abram,

"Know of a surety that thy seed shall be a stranger in a

*land that is not their's, and shall serve them; and they shall
afflict them four hundred years; And also that nation, whom
they shall serve, will I judge: and afterward shall they
come out with great substance. And thou shalt go to thy fathers in peace; thou shalt be buried in a good old age. But
in the fourth generation they shall come hither again: for
the iniquity of the Amorites is not yet full."—Gen. 15:13-16.*

Iniquity Full

In the four hundred years from this prophecy to the conquest of Canaan the iniquity of the Amorites filled up and
God destroyed the Amorites. And, you know, my friends, I
have gone around over this country preaching the Word of
God for more than three decades. I have gone up and down
the land from the lakes to the gulf and from the Atlantic to
the Pacific, back and forth, over and over again. I have
preached in forty-two states and in many foreign lands. I
have gone with my ears and my eyes and my mind open. I
have read the newspapers and the magazines and have kept
up with current events and I have studied the Word of God
and history. My friends, I believe the iniquity of America
is filling up. The only thing that could save the American
dream and preserve the things that have made this nation
great is a turning back to God through the Lord Jesus Christ.

If It Seem Evil

Now, if it seem evil unto you to serve Him choose from
the many other gods whom ye will serve. In order that you
might have a clear picture of the alternatives we face let us
notice some of the distinctives of the religion of Jesus
Christ. Some people may object to our calling Christianity
a religion. Strictly speaking, it is the only real religion.
Religion means "reconnect." Sin severed man from God.
Jesus Christ reconnects us to Him.

Pardon

Our God is the only God who can offer pardon to the sinner. Socrates said, "The honor of God does not permit Him to forgive sinners out of pity." Ritschl said, "God may forgive sinners but I do not see how He can do it." Years ago at the World's Fair in Chicago a Dr. Cook represented Christianity at the great council of religions. After the representative of each great world religion had extolled the virtues of his religion Dr. Cook rose and told the story of Lady Macbeth. He told how after the murder of Duncan Lady Macbeth, who had conspired to have him murdered, walked in her sleep and looking at her lily-white hand cried, "Out, damned spot! Out, I say!...Who would have thought the old man had so much blood in him?" Then she exclaimed, "Here's the smell of blood still: all the perfumes of Arabia will not sweeten this little hand. Oh, oh, oh!" Then turning to the representatives of all the great world religions Dr. Cook asked, "Ladies and gentlemen, is there anything in the religion of any one present that could take the stains from the hands and the guilt from the soul of Lady Macbeth?" They all had to shake their heads in the negative. Then he said, "I present to you a Saviour who can do this. The blood of Jesus Christ God's Son cleanses us from all sin" (I John 1:7).

Pardon! That is the highest dogma in the Christian's theology! That is written in blood upon every page of Old Testament history from the shedding of blood in the garden to procure robes for Adam and Eve until Jesus cried, "It is finished" on the cross of Calvary. The meaning of the whole story is PARDON. Listen to the apostles of Jesus preach!

Hear Simon Peter! "Repent ye therefore, and be converted, that your sins may be blotted out" (Acts 3:19). Hear John! "If we confess our sins, he is faithful and just to forgive us our sins, and to cleanse us from all unrighteousness" (I John 1:9). Hear James! "Let him know, that he which converteth the sinner from the error of his way shall save a soul from death, and shall hide a multitude of sins" (Jas. 5:20). Hear Paul! "And all things are of God, who hath reconciled us to himself by Jesus Christ, and hath given to us the ministry of reconciliation; To wit, that God was in Christ, reconciling the world unto himself, not imputing their trespasses unto them" (II Cor. 5:18,19).

Listen to the Christians sing! The theme of their song is Pardon.

> Who is a pard'ning God like Thee?
> Or who has grace so rich and free?
> Or who has grace so rich and free?
>
> Great God of wonders! all Thy ways
> Are matchless, God-like, and divine;
> But the fair glories of Thy grace
> More God-like and unrivaled shine,
> More God-like and unrivaled shine.

> To God be the glory, great things He hath done,
> So loved He the world that He gave us His Son,
> Who yielded His life an atonement for sin,
> And opened the Life-gate that all may go in.
>
> Praise the Lord, praise the Lord,
> Let the earth hear His voice!
> Praise the Lord, praise the Lord,
> Let the people rejoice!
> O come to the Father, thro' Jesus the Son,
> And give Him the glory, great things He hath done.

Let Buddhism, and Mohammedanism, and Laoism, and Jainism, and all the cults and theories, and councils, and systems, and religions bow down at the feet of Jesus and stack their laurels at the foot of His cross for they cannot pardon the sinner.

Makes Men Happy

Christ is the only God who can make men happy. He

makes us happy because He pardons from the guilt of sin,
delivers us from the power of sin and gives us assurance
that one day He will deliver us from the presence of sin.
Sin always causes sorrow and to be delivered from it is to
be made happy. Jesus Christ makes us happy because He
gives us assurance of the love of God. A heathen in the
heart of Africa may look up through the giant mahogany
trees at the starlit heavens and think, "There must be a
God and He must love us. He has provided for our needs."
But a mighty tornado comes twisting through the jungle,
pushing giant trees down upon his grass hut and kills his
babies, and he wonders, "Is it true that God loves people?"
He may conceive of a God of love but He has no assurance
that "God is love."

The Christian Knows

But the Christian knows that He is love. It has been dem-
onstrated at Calvary and declared to be so in the Word of
God. We not only know that God is love, but we are also
made happy by the knowledge that "all things work together
for good to them that love God, to them who are the called
according to his purpose" (Rom. 8:28).

Fellowship

Jesus makes us happy because He gives us fellowship with
others and with Himself and with His Heavenly Father. John
said, "That which we have seen and heard declare we unto
you, that ye also may have fellowship with us: and truly our
fellowship is with the Father, and with his Son Jesus Christ.
And these things write we unto you, that your joy may be
full" (I John 1:3,4).

Adapted to All

Not only is the religion of Jesus the only religion that can
pardon the sinner, and the only religion that can make us
happy, but it is also the only religion that is adapted to all

people. It is adapted to all people racially—white people, red people, brown people, yellow people, and black people. I traveled in Latin America with a friend who said he was left alone with an aborigine Indian in a room a thousand miles up the Amazon. They sat there in silence for a while, unable to speak each other's language. Neither of them seemed for a few minutes to know what to do. Then my friend said the Indian got up and faced my friend and smiled the most infectious smile he ever saw, formed a cross with his fingers, pointed to his heart and then pointed upward. My friend said he felt his soul strangely knit to the soul of that Indian.

The religion of Jesus Christ is adapted to all people socially. Christ can save a king and He can save his most lowly subject. It is adapted to all people circumstantially. He can save the rich and He can save the poor. It is adapted to people of every age. In Princeton, Indiana, one night I had an old man eighty-nine years of age converted. The same night I had a little nine-year-old boy saved. The next night I saw them talking together. The old man said, "Just think, Son, I have wasted eighty years since I was your age. I wish I had been saved when I was nine. But I sure am glad I was saved last night. This has been the happiest day of my life." The little boy said, "I am sure glad I was saved last night, too."

The religion of Jesus Christ is adapted to every age of the world's history. It was good for the "horse and buggy days." It was good for the automobile age. It is good for the jet and atomic age and it will be good for any other age yet to come. It was adapted to Adam and Eve wandering in their tunics of skin near the Garden of Eden and will be adapted to the last generation this side of the white throne judgment.

It is adapted to all people morally. Jesus Christ can save the moralist and He can save the wretch plunged into the deepest bogs of human depravity. It is adapted to all people intellectually. The profoundest scholars and most brilliant intellects are those that have been illuminated by the Spirit of God. And yet the "world by wisdom knew not God." "The natural man receiveth not the things of the Spirit of God... neither can he know them, because they are spiritually discerned."

It never disturbs me when a half-wit gives a testimony. Somebody may pull my coattail and say, "Don't let him testify. He will spoil the service." No, he will not hurt the service unless you turn it over to him. He has a testimony to give. Let him give his testimony and then sit down right quickly. Smart people say, "That is wonderful! Jesus can save a poor dimwit like that." He can save the moron and He can save the philosopher.

Not Only the Intelligentia

God does not put salvation up where only the intelligentia can get it. Ordinary people would have to go to Hell because the average person would be incapable of receiving salvation.

Power to Live It

The religion of the Lord Jesus Christ is the only religion that gives one the power to live up to its demands. The religions of the world say, "Do and live." Christianity says, "Live and do."

"So then they that are in the flesh cannot please God. But ye are not in the flesh, but in the Spirit, if so be that the Spirit of God dwell in you. Now if any man have not the Spirit of Christ, he is none of his."—Rom. 8:8,9.

I choose Jesus! Choose your god!

VIII

Out of the Night

SCRIPTURE READING: JOHN 3:1-16

In this message I am to demonstrate that because men are born sinners they need to be born again, that the new birth is a miracle wrought by the Holy Spirit incomprehensible to man but experienced by simple, childlike faith.

"There was a man of the Pharisees, named Nicodemus, a ruler of the Jews: The same came to Jesus by night."—John 3:1,2.

Nicodemus Came at Night

Evidently Nicodemus was troubled. It must have been that there was a lack in his soul, and he was conscious of the fact that he had come to Jesus at night. The craving in his soul was so intense he could not have waited until morning. There was a burning desire to know God. So he came to Jesus at night. There are those who tell us that Nicodemus came at night because he was afraid of persecution on the part of the Jews. Others tell us that he came at night because he was a busy man and did not have time to come through the day. There may be something to either one of these suggestions, but I believe he came because he wanted to know God. And he came to Him who is the way to God, and said, "Rabbi, we know that thou art a teacher come from God."

Blindness of the Natural Mind

Now everybody who comes to Jesus comes under the cover of darkness. It may not be physical darkness, but spiritual darkness. For every soul without the Lord Jesus

Christ is groping in the dark. If you are without Christ, you are groping in darkness as black as Hell's sable badge and pitchy scowl. Every soul without Christ is groping without light. "The natural man receiveth not the things of the Spirit of God: for they are foolishness unto him: neither can he know them, because they are spiritually discerned" (I Cor. 2:14). The unregenerate man cannot even understand the Christian, let alone the things of God.

Sometime ago I handed a man on the street corner a card and invited him to come out to special services. He tore up the card, threw it down and began to curse and blaspheme God. I said, "Friend, I feel sorry for you." I started down the street and he followed me a half block.

He said, "Wait a minute! Don't you feel sorry for me."
"Well," I said, "I can't help it. I feel sorry for you."
He said, "I feel sorry for you."
I said, "Thank you, sir. And I feel sorry for you."
He said, "Don't you feel sorry for me!"
I said, "I can't help it. I feel sorry for you, sir."
He said, "I feel sorry for you."
I said, "Friend, there was a time when I was outside the temple of salvation. I had never seen the inside of the temple, but one day, thank God, I entered this wonderful temple and have seen on the inside. I have seen outside and I have seen inside. You have never seen inside."

If you have not been born again you cannot see the things of God; you have no eyes with which to see. The man without God cannot see spiritual things.

Necessity of the New Birth

Jesus turned those soul-searching eyes into the heart of Nicodemus and said, "Except a man be born again, he cannot see the kingdom of God."

Nicodemus did not understand what He was talking about and said, "How can a man be born when he is old? can he enter the second time into his mother's womb, and be born?"

Jesus answered, "Verily, verily, I say unto thee...That which is born of the flesh is flesh." In other words, He said, "Nicodemus, I am not talking about the first birth. I am not talking about the natural birth. That which is born of the flesh is flesh. That is why you have to be born again. That which is born of the flesh is flesh."

Paul said, 'In my flesh dwells no good thing.' There is nothing good in you, in the flesh. There is nothing good in your flesh.

The Flesh Is Sinful

We read a great deal in our day about the spark of divinity in human nature. There is nothing divine about human nature. If there is anything divine about you it is because you, by simple faith, have accepted Jesus Christ as your personal Saviour; it is because you have received a new nature; it is because the Holy Spirit has wrought in you a new birth; the nature of Christ has been imparted to you and you have become a child of God by simple faith in Jesus Christ. But that which is born of the flesh is flesh. It cannot be anything else. It may be cultured flesh; it may be elegant flesh; it may be refined flesh; it may even be restrained flesh; it may join the church and be baptized, but it is flesh. It may be preaching flesh. There are preachers who have not been born again.

A Sinner May Preach

I was conducting a radio program in Philadelphia and was invited to come to a certain community nearby and preach one night. I went out and preached and the pastor came forward. He said, "I have never been born again, but I am going to take Jesus Christ as my personal Saviour. I have preached the new birth; I have preached Jesus; I have preached the Bible; but I have not been born again. In fact," he said, "I have depended upon my preaching and upon my good life and the things I knew, but I have not been born again. By the grace of God, tonight I am going to cast myself upon Jesus and Him alone."

A Sinner May Teach Sunday School

"That which is born of the flesh is flesh." It may be religious flesh. I was teaching Sunday school when I found Jesus Christ as my Saviour. I had never been born again. That morning it dawned on me that I needed Him. I was reading my Bible. I was studying Sunday school lessons. I was teaching Sunday school. I was living a good, decent life, but I did not have Jesus. I did not have life. What I am talking to you about is a miracle. I am saying to you that that which is born of the flesh and merely born of the flesh, is flesh. Nicodemus was a religious man. Nicodemus was a ruler of the Jews. He was a very religious man. But he needed to be born again.

Men Are Sinners

"All have sinned, and come short of the glory of God.... There is none righteous." Say, the fact of sin is a fact that I do not have to prove. Anybody who is willing to admit that life is real has to admit the fact of sin. The Holy Spirit convicts of this sin, that sin, and the other sin because people believe not on Jesus Christ. That is why they are in sin, because they believe not on Jesus. Somebody has said that it is not so much of a sin question as it is a Son question. That is true. It is a Son question. But the Spirit of God convicts men of particular sins because they believe not on Jesus Christ. I do not believe it is a matter of reformation. I do not believe it is a matter of cutting out this sin or that sin. I do not believe in just cutting the limbs off the tree of sin. That is not enough. It is not enough just to cut this out, then cut that out. The reason the fruits of sin grow on the tree of sin is that the tree has a sinful nature.

It depends upon what one is at heart. Sinners are not sinners because they sin; they sin because they are sinners. A Christian is not a Christian because he lives a Christian life; he lives a Christian life because he is a Christian at heart. That is why he needed to be born again.

A "Naturally-Born" Sinner

A young fellow, a defeated Christian, came to my office. He was a babe in Christ. He had taken some setbacks. He was a defeated Christian. He came in, sat down across the desk from me and started to cry. He dropped his head on my desk; I laid my hand on his shoulder across the table, and I said, "What is the matter, Son?"

He looked up at me: "Dr. Parker, I must be a naturally-born sinner."

I said, "You certainly are. That is exactly what you are. So am I. So is every Christian. And, of course, people who are not Christians are sinners. We are born sinners. 'That which is born of the flesh is flesh.' Born sinners! It is as natural for man to sin as it is for him to breathe. It is as natural for man to sin as it is for sparks to fly upward. You are a born sinner for you are born of the flesh. And all have sinned! All have completed the act of sinning! That is a certain Greek tense which denotes completed action. All have sinned. When Adam sinned, the human race sinned, and, therefore, all are coming short of the glory of God. That is why people need to be born again. They are sinners."

This young fellow was a defeated Christian. He said, "I am just a naturally-born sinner." I took the Word of God and pointed to Romans, the third chapter, and then I went to the seventh chapter. I took this passage and I said, "Now you listen; you follow me here." I turned it to him so he could see it. And I read, "When I would do good, evil is present with me. For I delight in the law of God after the inward man: But I see another law in my members, warring against the law of my mind, and bringing me into captivity to the law of sin which is in my members. O wretched man that I am!"

Backslider, the Most Miserable Person

It does not matter whether this passage is the expression of a man under the law trying to please God or a backslidden Christian realizing his defeat, it shows the weakness of the flesh and the utter despair of a man striving to please God in the flesh. The most wretched person in all the world is a Christian out of fellowship with Jesus Christ. He is more miserable than a person who never knew God. A Christian out of fellowship can never be happy without the will of God in his life. After you have known God, you can never be happy with sin. Somebody said, "Can a Christian sin?" He may sin, but he cannot enjoy it. He ought not to sin; he doesn't have to, and God says, 'I write these things unto you that you sin not' (I John 2:1). You don't have to sin, but if you do, you cannot enjoy it.

This fellow said, "Well, that is my picture. That is my trouble." Paul said, "O wretched man that I am! who shall deliver me from the body of this death?" And then it was as though he thought of the only One who is in the delivering business. He must have shouted with an exultant cry, or perhaps he pressed hard upon the parchment as he wrote: "I thank God through Jesus Christ...!" He is the Deliverer. He can deliver from the penalty of sin. He can deliver from the power of it. I do not have to be a defeated Christian. I can rise above the carnal. I can walk on a higher plane. I can have victory through Jesus Christ. As a preacher, as an evangelist, as a pastor, as a teacher, as an ordinary Christian, I can be separated unto the Gospel of Jesus Christ. There is where you will find your victory.

People are born sinners. Naturally, they are sinners. That is the thing that holds back the power, blocks revival, and thwarts the power of God in the life of a Christian.

I refuse to preach without the power of God. I will not do it! This job is too big. I had rather be anything—I had rather be a bootlegger; I had rather be a bookie than to be a preacher without power in my life. I had rather die a thousand times than to be a preacher without the power of God. I would do more good anywhere on earth than to stand in the pulpit like a dog in the manger.

What did Jesus say to those hypocrites? He said, "You whited sepulchres, you! You are full of rottenness within you. You are all white on the outside, but you are dogs in a manger." He didn't put it in those words, but He said, "Ye shut up the kingdom of heaven against men: for ye neither go in yourselves, neither suffer ye them that are entering to go in" (Matt. 23:13).

Fact of Sin

"That which is born of flesh is flesh." I do not have to prove that. You are guilty of sin. It is a fact of human experience. It is a fact of observation.

Down in Alabama one day a man rushed up on the porch of a home where I was visiting and said, "I heard a gun fire and someone screamed." We rushed across the street and there was the mute evidence of a suicide. There was a double-barrel shotgun on the floor and a walking cane with which the man evidently had pushed the trigger. A puddle of blood was on the floor and just over the hole where the full charge of the shot went through his heart, the man's shirt was powder burned. We had to wait for the coroner. Somebody said, "His wife was out of town and he was here alone." Somebody else said, "This was the bitter end of a sinful life." I looked at the expression on his dead face, at the horror written on his countenance. I stood there and I began to think, "The bitter end of a sinful life." I watched the red blood as it oozed from his heart and I saw it as it began to drip into a little puddle at his side. Drip! Drip! Drip! I tell you, my friends, it seemed to me that from every blighted life and every broken home and every wrecked virtue and from every home of squalor and want, and from every prison cell and from every battlefield, from all the scourges of humanity caused by sin, there arose to God the piteous cry: "How long, O God? How long will sin curse us? How long will sin crush and damn and blight?"

Sin Is to Blame

Sin has blighted the world. You had as well say war has never raged as to say there is no sin. You had as well say there is no suffering, there is no sorrow, as to say there is no sin, because sin always causes sorrow in the heart of an individual, or in the life of a nation. Collectively or individually, sin brings sorrow. Of course, the innocent suffer with the guilty, for the guilty, on account of the guilty, and more than the guilty, oftentimes, but sin causes sorrow.

I was in Detroit holding a meeting some years ago and a man came forward one night and went to the inquiry room. He said, "I am the world's champion professional ski jumper. Last winter I fell on skis and was badly injured. I was reared a Christian Scientist. From the time I was a little child I was taught that there was no such thing as pain. I was also taught there was no such thing as sin, but if a man sinned, he just thought he sinned. He did not actually sin. He was just in error, that was all. He just had the wrong outlook on things. If he thought he was hurt, he was just in error. He was not actually hurt."

This reminded me of the little boy who said, "Mother, you know the sick lady down the street?" She said, "The lady who thinks she is sick, darling." "Well," he said, "she thinks she is dead now."

The ski jumper said, "I was badly hurt. They came to my bedside and told me I was in error." He said, "That fall broke the spell of hypnosis. I could no longer kid myself about it. I had to admit that pain was real. But when I was willing to admit that pain was real, I had to admit the fact of sin." He said, "I am so glad I came here tonight and heard the Gospel story how Jesus Christ died to save me from sin." I had the joy of leading that man to Christ.

Symptoms of the Disease

You can't get around the fact of sin. It is an awful fact. Now, of course, our business is not merely to tear down; it if not merely to point out sin. Special sins are symptoms of a disease. Men do not go to Hell for committing murder. They commit murder because they are going to Hell. Men do not go to Hell for stealing. They steal because their hearts are not right and because they are going to Hell. Men do not go to Hell for dancing. They may block some-body else and send somebody else to Hell, and dancing may involve worse sins, but people do not go to Hell for dancing. They live sinful lives because they are sinners. They do these things because they are not born again.

God's Diagnosis of Man

God lays man out on an examining table and looks him over as a physician diagnoses a patient. He says, "From the sole of the foot even unto the head there is no soundness in it; but wounds, and bruises, and putrifying sores: they have not been closed, neither bound up, neither mollified with ointment" (Isa. 1:6). He x-rays man's brain and says, "There is none that understandeth, there is none that seek-eth after God. They are all gone out of the way, they are together become unprofitable; there is none that doeth good, no, not one" (Rom. 3:11,12).

He turns a light into the throat and says, "Their throat is an open sepulchre." He looks at the tongue and writes on the chart, "With their tongues they have used deceit." He pulls back the lip and looks under it and records, "The poison of asps is under their lips" (Rom. 3:13). He takes another look into the mouth and says, "Whose mouth is full of cursing and bitterness" (Rom. 3:14).

He looks at the feet and declares, "Their feet are swift to shed blood: Destruction and misery are in their ways: And the way of peace have they not known" (Rom. 3:15-17).

He examines the eyes and says, "There is no fear of God before their eyes" (Rom. 3:18). He gets out His stethoscope and listens to man's heartbeat. He gives him a cardiogram. He says, "The heart is deceitful above all things, and desperately wicked: who can know it?" (Jer. 17:9). Literally: "A Jacob is the heart as distinguished from all else, and is malignant: who can know it?" The Physician just shakes His head and declares, "For all have sinned, and come short of the glory of God" (Rom. 3:23). And then He says, "The wages of sin is death" (Rom. 6:23).

"Then," someone asks, "is there no hope for man?"

"Just one," says the Physician, "That is for man to be born again. The first time he was born he was born of the flesh. His only hope is to be born of the Spirit. 'That which is born of the flesh is flesh; and that which is born of the Spirit is spirit.'"

"Is there no balm in Gilead; is there no physician there? why then is not the health of the daughter of my people recovered?" (Jer. 8:22). Thank God there is a Physician and there is a remedy! The blood of Jesus Christ, God's Son, cleanseth us from all sin. "That which is born of the Spirit is spirit. Marvel not that I said unto thee, Ye must be born again."

The Remedy

Well, there is the remedy—the new birth. "Ye must be born again." Now you do not have to understand it. Nicodemus did not understand. He said, "How can a man be born when he is old? can he enter the second time into his mother's womb, and be born?" Jesus explained it and said in effect, "Nicodemus, you do not understand how the wind blows. You feel it on your cheek; you hear the leaves rustle out yonder, you see the grass as it bows in the wind.

You do not know where the wind is coming from; you do not know where it is going. And if you cannot understand the wind, how do you expect to understand the mighty moving of Him of whom the wind is merely a type, the Holy Spirit? You cannot understand it."

A Miracle

Nobody really understands it. It is a miracle. Knowledge will not bring it about. An understanding of it will not do it. You do not find God in your head. "The world by wisdom knew not God." You cannot find God by searching.

No Man Hath Ascended to Heaven

Jesus said, "And no man hath ascended up to heaven, but he that came down from heaven, even the Son of man which is in heaven." He was not teaching here that nobody had gone to Heaven after death; although it is believed that Old Testament saints went into Paradise, a compartment in Hades, to await the resurrection of Christ and their transferral to Heaven. Jesus was teaching that men do not go to Heaven to get acquainted with God. You cannot ascend to Heaven by your own power. We may shoot rockets into the sky and even to outer space, but we cannot make it by this means to the Heaven of heavens where God sits upon the throne of this universe. You cannot climb to Heaven on a ladder of logic. You cannot vault to Heaven on a pole of philosophy. You cannot rocket to Heaven in a missile of reason. Men do not go up there to meet God. He came down from Heaven in the Person of Jesus Christ to introduce Himself to mankind.

Not by Knowledge

You do not come to God through the intellect. Of course, it is all right to be able to give a reason for the hope that is within you, "upset the other fellow's applecart," and all that sort of thing when he gives us excuses, but you do not win

men to God by argument. If the Holy Spirit does not bring
conviction, there is no hope for them. And if you proclaim
the Gospel of Jesus Christ, the whole counsel of God, and do
not trim your sails, God will send that Gospel forth in power. It is never preached in the Spirit when there is no conviction. Men do not find God by reason. The Gospel is not
reasonable to an unreasonable man. And a person cannot
reason about spiritual things until he has light from God.
He may be able to go into the intricacies of Biblical teaching. He may know theology. I have sat at the feet of men
who knew theology in great theological seminaries, brilliant
men who knew the theories of the masters of the ages in
theology, but they did not know God.

In a certain theological seminary where I once studied in
New York I sat at the feet of a brilliant man, a man who
knew everything. He knew the orthodox position. One day
he stood up and said, "We modernists have drenched the
world in blood. We are responsible for World War II. We
have taken the people astray. We are guilty. We stand with
our fingers dripping with the blood of the peoples of the
world. We have departed far from the old fundamental position. We have gone astray. What we need to do is to re-
trace our steps back in the direction of the old position,
back to the place where we can form a synthesis with the
orthodox position. What we need is a NEW modernism." I
heard him say it! In other words, "We played the fool once;
what we need to do is to play the fool again!"

I once heard an old preacher talking to a group of college
students say, "Blessed is the student who does not play the
fool. For verily, verily, I say unto thee, he that playeth the
fool two or three times close together becomes one."

Men play the fool because they are fools. I talked to a
young fellow. He said, "I am an agnostic, and you are a
Christian. You accept it by faith; I have to have proof for
it. We can't know whether there is a God."

"How can we prove anything to you if you cannot know?"
I asked.

"Well," he said, "we cannot know anything."

I said, "Do you know anything?"

He said, "No."

I said, "I didn't think so. Then you don't know that I don't
know anything. That is just a theory with you. You don't
know that we cannot know anything."

There was a philosopher back yonder—a 'foolosopher,'
by the name of Descartes. He doubted everything. He
doubted that he existed. One day he said, "There is one
thing I cannot doubt; I cannot doubt that I doubt. If I doubt,
I must exist, and if I exist, everything else must be real."
So he built up a positive philosophy. But this fellow said,
"You can't know anything. And yet," he said, "your trouble is that you are not scientific."

"What is science?" I asked.

He said, "It is classified knowledge." Agnosticism—the
Greek *a* means "without"; *gnosko*—I know; *agnosko*—I know
not. Agnostic—one who knows not. It is the same as the
Latin word *ignoramus*. But he said you can't know anything.

"Are you a scientist or an agnostic?" I asked.

"Well," he said, "in the realm of the material, I am a
scientist, but in the realm of the spiritual, I am an agnostic."

Try Jesus

I said, "Why don't you take Jesus Christ into your labora-
tory and put Him to the test and try to see if He is what He
claims to be? Apply scientific principles to Jesus. Put Him
to the test. 'The proof of the pudding is in the eating.' 'Try
me now,' says God.

Philip said to Nathanael, "Come and see."

That is my challenge: Come and see. Just try God. If
you want power, you try God. You just cut loose and cast
yourself upon Him. If you want power in your life as a

minister, as an evangelist, you try God. You meet the conditions. You do what God tells you to do and see if God does not do His part.

Faith, the Principle of Regeneration

Because men are born sinners they need to be born again. The new birth is a miracle wrought by the Holy Spirit. Man cannot understand it but may experience it by simple, child-like faith.

Complete Trust

Unsaved friend here tonight, why don't you believe in Jesus? Why don't you cast yourself upon Jesus? Do you know what it means to do that? Just do it! Suppose I fall from the top of a cliff and in my fall I seize a vine growing out of a crevice in the side of a cliff and I swing to the vine, but the vine begins to break. It snaps yonder and yonder and yonder, and there is only one strand holding—just one vine. It begins to crack. I fall a few feet. I begin to pray. I look up and it is hundreds of feet to where the light breaks over the cliff top. I look down into the abyss and it is hundreds of feet yonder to those jagged rocks beneath. I reach out to the side and there is nothing to hold to. I reach to the other side; there is nothing there but the bare wall of a boulder. So I hang onto the vine and pray for dear life: "O God, save me! Save me!" As soon as I open my eyes, I see an angel with broad wings and strong arms and a smiling face. I cry to the angel, "Save me!"

The angel says, "Do you believe I will save you?"

I say, "Yes, I believe you will save me." I connect the fact that he came just as I needed him, and my prayer and that smiling countenance and his questions. I say, "Yes, I know you will save me."

He says, "I will if you will trust me. Turn loose the vine, and I will catch you ere you are dashed on the rocks below."

That is what it means to trust Jesus. It means to turn

loose every feeble effort to save yourself; it means to turn
loose every support; it means to trust Christ and Christ
alone. And not until you trust Christ like that will the work
of the new birth take place. Not until you cast yourself upon Him and trust not church, nor baptism, nor good works—
as proper as all these things are for Christian people—can
you be saved. Trust Christ!

The very moment you trust Jesus Christ you become a
new creation. The miracle of the new birth transpires.
You become a child of God. A new nature—the nature of
Christ is imparted to you. You can never be the same.
"Being born again, not of corruptible seed, but of incorrupt-
ible, by the word of God, which liveth and abideth for ever"
(I Pet. 1:23).

What about baptism and church membership? What about
obedience to God, a holy walk, and a righteous life? It is
normal for these to follow the new birth. We are not saved
by faith and works but we are saved by faith that works.
"He which hath begun a good work in you will perform it
until the day of Jesus Christ." Trust the Saviour now and
this miracle will transpire.

IX

A Bride for Isaac

"And he said, I am Abraham's servant. And the Lord hath blessed my master greatly; and he is become great: and he hath given him flocks, and herds, and silver, and gold, and menservants, and maidservants, and camels, and asses. And Sarah my master's wife bare a son to my master when she was old: and unto him hath he given all that he hath. And my master made me swear saying, Thou shalt not take a wife to my son of the daughters of the Canaanites, in whose land I dwell: But thou shalt go unto my father's house, and to my kindred, and take a wife unto my son. And I said unto my master, Peradventure the woman will not follow me. And he said unto me, The Lord, before whom I walk, will send his angel with thee, and prosper thy way; and thou shalt take a wife for my son of my kindred, and of my father's house: Then shalt thou be clear from this my oath, when thou comest to my kindred; and if they give not thee one, thou shalt be clear from my oath.

"And I came this day unto the well, and said, O Lord God of my master Abraham, if now thou do prosper my way which I go: Behold, I stand by the well of water; and it shall come to pass, that when the virgin cometh forth to draw water, and I say to her, Give me, I pray thee, a little water of thy pitcher to drink; And she say to me, Both drink thou, and I will also draw for thy camels: let the same be the woman whom the Lord hath appointed out for my master's son. And before I had done speaking in mine heart, behold, Rebekah came forth with her pitcher on her shoulder; and she went down unto the well, and drew water: and I said unto her, Let me drink, I pray thee. And she made haste, and let down her pitcher from her shoulder, and said, Drink, and I will give thy camels drink also: so I drank, and she made the camels drink also. And I asked her, and said, Whose daughter art thou? And she said, The daughter

of Bethuel, Nahor's son, whom Milcah bare unto him: and I put the earring upon her face, and the bracelets upon her hands. And I bowed down my head, and worshipped the Lord, and blessed the Lord God of my master Abraham, which had led me in the right way to take my master's brother's daughter unto his son. And now if ye will deal kindly and truly with my master, tell me: and if not, tell me; that I may turn to the right hand, or to the left.

"Then Laban and Bethuel answered and said, The thing proceedeth from the Lord: we cannot speak unto thee bad or good. Behold, Rebekah is before thee, take her, and go, and let her be thy master's son's wife, as the Lord hath spoken.

"And it came to pass, that, when Abraham's servant heard their words, he worshipped the Lord, bowing himself to the earth. And the servant brought forth jewels of silver, and jewels of gold, and raiment, and gave them to Rebekah: he gave also to her brother and to her mother precious things. And they did eat and drink, he and the men that were with him, and tarried all night; and they rose up in the morning, and he said, Send me away unto my master.

"And her brother and her mother said, Let the damsel abide with us a few days, at the least ten; after that she shall go. And he said unto them, Hinder me not, seeing the Lord hath prospered my way; send me away that I may go to my master. And they said, We will call the damsel, and inquire at her mouth. And they called Rebekah, and said unto her, Wilt thou go with this man?

"And she said, I will go. And they sent away Rebekah their sister, and her nurse, and Abraham's servant, and his men. And they blessed Rebekah, and said unto her, Thou art our sister, be thou the mother of thousands of millions, and let thy seed possess the gate of those that hate them. And Rebekah arose, and her damsels, and they rode upon the camels, and followed the man: and the servant took Rebekah, and went his way.

"And Isaac came from the way of the well Lahai-roi; for he dwelt in the south country. And Isaac went out to meditate in the field at the eventide: and he lifted up his eyes, and saw, and behold, the camels were coming. And Rebekah

lifted up her eyes, and when she saw Isaac, she lighted off the camel. For she had said unto the servant, What man is this that walketh in the field to meet us? And the servant had said, It is my master: therefore she took a vail, and covered herself. And the servant told Isaac all things that he had done. And Isaac brought her into his mother Sarah's tent, and took Rebekah, and she became his wife; and he loved her: and Isaac was comforted after his mother's death."—Gen. 24:34-67.

Types

I know it is possible for us to push typology too far, and set things forth as types when they are not really intended by God to be illustrations of other truths. But I am going to draw an analogy from this 24th chapter of Genesis. I would not say that every illustration I find here is actually a divinely purposed illustration.

Isaac

At least Isaac is a type of Jesus in that he was offered as a sacrifice on Mount Moriah, for we are told so in the eleventh chapter of Hebrews. But in several ways Isaac is a wonderful illustration of the Lord Jesus Christ. He was born of a miracle when Sarah was more than ninety years of age. The Lord Jesus was virgin-born. When Isaac was a young man he was offered as a sacrifice on a mountain. As Christ was raised from the dead so Isaac was delivered from this death by the miraculous intervention of the angel of God who cried out and told Abraham not to lay his hand upon Isaac. Isaac went back to his father's home after he was offered as a sacrifice on a mountain. And the next picture we have of him is when he goes out to meditate in the field in the evening. He lifts up his eyes, and behold, the camels are coming. Rebekah alights from the camel and rushes to meet him. He takes her into his mother's tent and loves her and she becomes his wife, and he is comforted after his mother's death.

Jesus Christ

When the Lord Jesus Christ ascended on high after His crucifixion, He sat down at the right hand of God the Father. The Holy Spirit was sent into the world to woo and win for Christ a bride. The Lord Jesus did not come back to win His own bride. I have often wondered what the results would have been had the Lord Jesus Christ remained here and preached. Of course, it was necessary for Him to sit down at the right hand of the Father as our great High Priest, to make intercession for us. But I have often wondered what kind of results He would have got if He had gone around with His nail-pierced hands and His thorn-torn brow and preached. But that was not the Father's will. Just as Abraham said, "Beware thou that thou bring not my son thither again," it was not the will of the Father for Isaac to go back to the land where Abraham had lived, back to Mesopotamia, to win his own bride. The servant was sent for that purpose.

Plan for Evangelization

I heard Dr. S. D. Gordon, in one of his "Quiet Talks," tell a legend. He said that when Jesus ascended on high, the angels gathered around to praise Him and to talk with Him about the great task He had accomplished. One of them said, "What plan do you have for the evangelization of the world?" Jesus said, "I told a few disciples about the future plan of the ages. And I told a few disciples what I would have them do. I gave them the commission to go out and preach the Gospel to all people. I left it in the hands of my disciples." One of the angels, perhaps the Archangel Michael, said, "Suppose the disciples fail?" And the Lord said, "I have no other plan."

Of course, that is just a legend, but that is God's plan for evangelizing the world. He told the disciples to take the message out to the people. But the Holy Spirit came to woo and to win for Christ a bride. You and I are the ones through whom the Holy Spirit is accomplishing this work.

Christians Soul Winners

Every Christian is called to be a soul winner. We are the ones through whom the Spirit of God is winning the bride. We are members of the bride. Of course, that is figurative. We are also members of the church, and we are members of the body of Jesus Christ. That is figurative language. We are not literally the bride of Jesus. We are the brethren of Christ. Actually, we are born into God's family and we are His brethren, bound to Him by the bonds of indestructible kinship. We are the sons of God and He has sent the Spirit of His Son into our hearts whereby we cry, "Abba, Father." But when the Bible represents the church as being the bride of Jesus, that is figurative language, because we are also members of His temple, we are living stones, we are members of His body, and we are members of His bride. He is wooing from the world a bride, but He is doing so through you and me. And the Holy Spirit, using the Word of God, working through men of God, is doing the work of God. It is our task to win men unto Jesus Christ. In this age God's purpose is to gather out from among the nations a people for His name. That was determined at the first church council in Jerusalem. After Paul and Barnabas had been on their missionary journey, they came back and reported to the church at Antioch which had sent them out the work they had done and how God had blessed them. And they began to discuss the Gentiles who had come into the church. Somebody said that these Gentile converts would have to become proselyte Jews and then they could be received into full fellowship. They decided to seek the counsel of the apostles and elders in the church at Jerusalem. It was determined that it was wrong to put them under the law. James got up and made a speech and said, "Men and brethren, hearken unto me: Simeon hath declared [i.e., Simon Peter] how God at the first did visit the Gentiles [or

for the first time; when he went over to Cornelius with the
Gospel for the first time], to take out of them a people for
his name.... After this I will return, and will build again
the tabernacle of David, which is fallen down; and I will
build again the ruins thereof, and I will set it up: That the
residue of men might seek after the Lord." So in this age
God is calling out from the nations of the world a people for
His name.

The Called-Out

The Spirit of God is calling out a people for the name of
Christ. And the word "church" itself, *ekklesia*, means "the
called-out." We are called out as members of His body and
members of His bride. The work of a local church is to win
people to Jesus Christ, baptize them, teach them all things
commanded and send them out to do the same thing. So we
can say that the ultimate purpose of a true church is to win
souls. "The chief end of man is to glorify God and to enjoy
Him forever" (Westminster Catechism). But God's ultimate
purpose for the churches is to gather out a people for His
name. We, as churches, and as individual Christians, are
the ones through whom God is carrying out this work.

Helper of God

We are told in Genesis 15:2 that the steward of Abraham's
house was "Eliezer of Damascus." The name Eliezer means
"helper of God." We are servants and helpers of God.
Now, since we have the same responsibility Eliezer had,
the obtaining for our Master a bride, and since Eliezer had
such good success, let us learn his methods for our own
use.

He Was Prayerful

In the first place, the man was prayerful. He said, "O
Lord God of my master Abraham, if now thou do prosper
my way which I go: Behold, I stand by the well of water."

He was prayerful. He prayed about it, and he had definite leadership in answer to prayer. You have to stay in touch with God and with His Spirit if you are going to be led of the Spirit of God.

He Was Spirit-Led

But this man was successful in the work that he did because he was Spirit-led. I read of a man who stood on the street corner in gay, sinful Paris and cried, "God loves you! God loves you!" until the Holy Spirit struck conviction to the hearts of people on the street, and the great All Mission Work of France was started. The secret is that the Spirit of God prompted the man to do that. God does not want every Christian to go out on the street and cry out, "God loves you!" But He wants you to work in your own individual way. But that man had the Spirit of God upon him. I read of a man who went down a busy street in Chicago and suddenly he was impressed to speak to a stranger about his soul. The stranger said, "I am running from God now." He said, "If you will go with me to a certain tabernacle I will accept the Lord Jesus Christ as my Saviour." The secret of that is that the Spirit of God led that man.

He Was in God's Will

Abraham's servant said, "I being in the way, the Lord led me to the house of my master's brethren....to take my master's brother's daughter unto his son." He was in the way. He was in the will of God. He could be led of God.

I could tell you some wonderful stories of how God led so definitely. One day I spoke to a man and led him to Jesus Christ. He told me about his lost brother and asked me to pray for him. That very afternoon I contacted another fellow and led him to Christ. After he had made his decision, we began to talk and I found that this was the brother for whom the other man had asked me to pray. The Spirit of God was leading in that. Definitely He was leading, working it out. Abraham's servant was in the will of God and God could lead him. And if you and I will place ourselves in the will of God, we will be used of God, we will be active but we will be passive in the hands of the Holy Spirit. The secret of successful soul winning is to be dominated and controlled and directed by the Holy Spirit. He does miraculous things with Christian people and leads us in miraculous ways in soul winning for Jesus Christ.

He Was Practical

This man was practical. He was out for a damsel, so he went to the path of the damsels of the city. He stood outside the city by a well of water at the time that women go out to draw water. If I were going fishing, I would not be as Simple Simon—"go a fishin'" in my mother's pail. I would go out where the fish are, go out to the river, out to the lake. I would not drop a hook in a bucket of water.

The day has long since passed when we can ring a church bell and expect sinners to come flocking in in droves saying, "What must we do to be saved?" The day has long passed when you can hang out a shingle and say, "Revival Meeting," and expect multitudes to come flocking in. Nothing will draw a crowd and hold people and keep on holding them like the preaching of the Word of God. "It pleased God by the foolishness of preaching to save them that believe." And nothing will take the place of preaching, old-fashioned gospel preaching. There is nothing that will hold people and attract people and keep on attracting people like preaching. Oh, you can draw a great crowd for a political rally or some other great mass meeting, but you can't keep on holding the crowd night after night with anything like you can with the preaching of the Word of God. But if we are going to reach people, we have to go out after them.

We read that the early church was scattered abroad and went everywhere preaching the Gospel except the apostles. They were in Jerusalem instructing the laymen and the laywomen, all the saints, and sending them out. They were going into the homes of the people, onto the street corners, into the open forum and into the marketplace, and everywhere preaching the Gospel. You talk about mass evangelism. I believe in mass evangelism in the sense that we set up a tent or tabernacle or come together in a great auditorium with a united effort of the Christian people of a community. We come together and bring the unsaved there and get them converted. I believe in that kind of mass evangelism. I am an evangelist. I spend all my time at it. All the time I can possibly give to that type of evangelism, I give it. The other time I am trying to make evangelists out of others. My heart and my life are on the altar of evangelism, and I believe in that kind of mass evangelism. But if we are going to reach the people, we have to go after them, we have to send our people out after them to bring them in.

Talking about mass evangelism: I remember once when I taught the famous preachers' class at Bob Jones University with a thousand ministerial students in the class—we were talking about this business of personal work and how God would lead. I told the preacher boys some old experiences I had years before. Thank God, I have some fresh ones to tell, too! But I was telling the boys about some wonderful past experiences, how one time when I was a student in college I was hitchhiking. I caught a ride out of the little town of Milton, Florida, going over to Pensacola. A few miles from town the fellow with whom I was riding said, "This is as far as I am going," and he turned off through the piney woods. I got out on the highway. It was a poor spot to catch a ride. Never get on a downgrade if you are trying to catch a ride. It was a long downgrade. I stood there and directed traffic for half an hour or so! I decided maybe I had too many bags, so I put one of my suitcases in the weeds and left a little handbag out on the highway, and kept on directing traffic. A car would pass with just one person in it—the driver, and I would show him the direction to Pensacola, but nobody stopped. I began to pray that God would stop somebody. I promised the Lord I would speak to that individual about his soul if the Lord would just cause him to stop and pick me up. While I was walking around praying and showing the people the right direction to go, I looked over in the woods and saw about 200 yards from the road eight fellows sawing logs. I wondered if I would have time to go over there and speak to those men. But I was afraid I might miss a ride, so I threw up my thumb again to let another fellow by. Then I decided that perhaps God wanted me to speak to those fellows.

Putting the little handbag in the weeds with my suitcase, I went across the highway, over into the woods, down where the men were working, walked up to them, took out my little New Testament and said, "Pardon me, gentlemen, but while I was standing over there on the highway waiting for the fellow to come along with whom I am going to ride to Pensacola, I saw you working over here. I thought you would not mind stopping for just a few minutes and let me tell you something wonderful." They put down their crosscut saws. I said, "Why don't you sit down there?" They sat down on the logs they were sawing. I said, "I will tell you what I am going to do. I am a preacher. How many of you fellows go to church? Do you go to church? Raise your hand." Nobody raised his hand. I said, "Well, let's have a little service. You don't go to church and you never get a chance to hear any preaching. Let's have a little service out here. I won't take but a few minutes." They said it was all right. I said, "Well, we don't have any choir, nor any instruments, but let's sing something. Do any of you know that old song, 'Love Lifted Me'?" Two of them said they did.

I "heisted" the tune and we sang the first stanza and the chorus. I stopped and said, "I know that song is true because I was sinking deep in sin, far from the peaceful shore, very deeply stained within, sinking to rise no more. But the

Master of the sea heard my despairing cry; from the waters lifted me and now safe am I. You know, fellows, sin is the only thing that ever causes sorrow. I know because I have tasted of sin." I gave my testimony and read a few verses from the Testament. I said, "How many of you fellows are Christians?" Not a one! I said, "Would you like to accept the Lord Jesus Christ?" One fellow said, "Yes." I could hardly believe it, you know, but I said, "All right, God bless you! Do you mean it?" "Yes, I mean it." Well, I thought he was too easy, too easy to win. I said, "Are you sure you want to trust Jesus?" Yes, he was. Tears came into his eyes and he fell down on his knees, turned around, put his arms over that old log, and the other fellows began to fall on their knees. We had eight penitents—the whole congregation—kneeling at that log! We turned that log into a mourner's bench! God was there. We had a revival out there in the woods. I know the Spirit led me in that. I know He did!

Mass Evangelism

We were talking about such things as that for several weeks there in the preachers' class. One of the fellows came to me and said, "Say, we have just got to go out and win souls. Most of us get out and do some preaching, but we have got to have some experiences like that." He said, "A large number of us are going out this week in cars to win some souls." They went over into a little community called Whitwell, Tennessee, and came back and said they had won over two hundred souls. They reported it in the preachers' class and all the boys were enthusiastic about it. They said, "We want to go." They organized a motor-cade—I forget how many carloads. Nearly 300 fellows went to Copper Hill, Tennessee, and Ducktown, two little communities together over in the copper bowl. They went in like a plague of grasshoppers, and stopped people on the streets. They went out and reached the whole town and came back and reported 623 souls!

That is the way the early church did. They went out and reached the people. It is important to preach the Word of God from the pulpit. I am so glad to have the emphasis on preaching. I believe in it. Let us not forget, however, that our business is to go out and get the people and reach them. Revival does that. When God's people get right with God, they go out and win souls for Jesus Christ.

Now this man was practical all right. Rebekah came with a pitcher on her shoulder. The servant asked God for a token of His leadership. You have a right to a token of God's leadership. We don't run on signs. We are not living in that day.

Tokens of Leadership

One night I was sitting on the platform in a church in Detroit praying that God would give me power as I preached. I said, "Lord, give me power tonight." I said, "You are going to be with me, Lord. You have never failed to be with me since the first time I preached." I don't know why I did a thing as childish as this, but I said, "Lord, will you be with me tonight? Will you be with me? Give me a sign that you are going to bless us tonight." I could not wait to see; I wanted a sign. I saw a little, short fellow come in, a little, duck-legged fellow, and I said, "Now, Lord, let a big, tall fellow come in if you are going to bless us tonight." Suddenly the passage came to me, "Lo, I am with you alway, even unto the end of the world" (Matt. 28:20). I said, "Never mind about the tall fellow, Lord. I don't need him. We have the Word of God." We don't need signs. We don't run on signs today. But you have a right to ask God for a token of His leadership and His blessing.

The Damsel Fair

So the man asked God for a token. Rebekah came with a

pitcher upon her shoulder. She was very fair to look upon, of course. She was a type of the bride of which our Lord said in the Song of Solomon, "Behold, thou art fair, my love; behold, thou art fair" (Song of Sol. 4:1). The servant said, "Would you give me a drink of water?" She said, "Why, of course. And I will draw water for your camels." She had a tender heart. She ran to the well and drew water for the camels. The man wondered at her but held his peace. He had jewels of silver and gold. He gave her bracelets and a nose ring. "Earring" is used in the King James Version, but it was a nose ring. They wore nose rings in those days. You perhaps have wondered why it stated "earring" and not "earrings": it was one nose ring. He gave her a nose ring and some bracelets. I like to think of that nose ring as earrings, you know, because they are more up-to-date. Anyhow, she had these jewels of gold. He said, "Is there room in your father's house for us to lodge in?" She answered, "Yes, and room for the camels, too." She was interested in those camels. She ran ahead of the man to prepare the way. She ran in and said, "Oh, Laban, look at my lovely bracelets! Look at my nose ring!"

Laban took it. You know, he was related to a certain people, and he said, "Vell, that looks like fourteen karat. Vere is the man?"

She said, "Down at the well."

"Vell," he said, "get things ready and I will go out and invite him in." He was very hospitable. He ran down to the man at the well and said, "Come in, thou blessed of the Lord. Wherefore standest thou without?" They came to the house. They wore barefoot sandals and traveled through the desert. So there was set water before them to wash their feet. They came into the house and sat down, let us imagine, at a table. Perhaps they sat on the floor in that old Bedouin home. We will imagine Laban said, "Vill you return thanks?" And he thanked God for journeying mercies and the hospitality of the home and said "Amen" to his prayer. Laban said, "Will you have a lamb chop?"

He said, "No, thank you."

Laban said, "Will you have some potatoes?"

"No, thank you."

"Aren't you hungry?"

"Very hungry. I am going to eat, but not now. I have something so much more important."

"Oh, we will talk business after supper. Have a hot biscuit."

"No, thank you."

"Now, come on and eat. We will talk later."

The servant said, "I cannot eat. I have something on my heart."

It didn't happen just like that, but that is what happened. There was set meat before him to eat, but he said, "I cannot eat until I have told mine errand."

A Passion

My friend, there is the secret of the man's success. He was dominated with a passion that would not let him eat until he had told his errand. If you and I who are called by the name of Christ and called to win souls to Jesus Christ, were so dominated with a passion, that we would say, "We can't eat! We can't stop to satisfy ourselves until we have done the work of Him who sent us. We cannot gratify our own desires until we have done the will of God," God would send a revival that would sweep America. I am not talking just about eating. I am not talking about fasting. It might not hurt us to fast sometimes and spend hours in prayer and fasting, but I am not talking about that. I am talking about putting first things first. If we were so dominated with a passion that we would say, "We won't take care of ourselves; we will take care of this job; we will do this work; we will win souls; we will sacrifice. We will give our time to it. We will spend time on our knees. We will put energy into it. We will spend money to do it. We will not satisfy ourselves. We will not gratify our desires. We won't think more of the middle part of our anatomy than we do of winning souls to Jesus Christ"—if you and I were dominated with a passion like that, I say, God would send a revival that would sweep America. If the evangelists whose lives are on the altar of evangelism, who have religion, who see the vision, who know that people are going to Hell if they do not have Jesus; and if the pastors who believe like these evangelists were so dominated that they would take the same attitude, and if people who are evangelistically-minded would let the passion grip them, God would send a revival. I do not mean a pretty good stir or awakening in some community—I mean a revival, a great turning back to God—if we had that passion.

I read in Dr. George Truett's book, *A Quest for Souls*, of a criminal sentenced to be hanged. A personal worker talked to him and the old criminal said, "Man, if I believed as you believe, that if I die without faith in Jesus Christ I would be lost and lost forever, I would be willing to crawl on my knees and tell people to repent and turn to God before it is too late." I do believe it. You believe it. We believe that if people die without Jesus Christ, they are lost forever. I say, God make us willing, if necessary, to crawl on our knees and tell people to repent and turn to God before it is too late.

Sincerity Respected

I have just scratched the surface of this chapter. They called Rebekah and said, "Will you go with this man?" But first they said, "All right, speak on." I tell you, when they see you have a passion burning in your soul, they may not accept your message, but they will listen to it. They will prick up their ears and they will listen. So he made his speech.

The Master Exalted

Suppose he got up and said, "I am the chief servant of Abraham. He never does anything important without consulting me. I am the elder servant of his household. He has great wealth, too, and it is all in my charge—cattle, silver, gold, menservants, maidservants, camels and asses—I have charge of all that wealth." Suppose he said, "Abraham called me in and said, 'Eliezer, I am thinking about my son's marriage.'" No, he didn't talk like that. He got up and said, "I am Abraham's servant. The Lord hath blessed my master greatly. God has given him menservants and maidservants and camels and asses." He exalted his master and his son. With the Holy Ghost, it is Jesus, Jesus, Jesus Christ the Son, who has preeminence. And the Spirit of God takes the things of Christ and shows them.

The Decision

And so they called Rebekah and said, "Wilt thou go?" She said, "I will." The Spirit only wins willing souls to the Lord Jesus. "I will go." It was settled. So they started. Down through the desert, down to the south country. The south country over there was like our Florida, the land of sunshine and flowers.

The Hard Journey

It was not an easy journey. It was through a desert on a camel's back. That is a difficult way to ride. Did you ever smell a camel? Well, the journey was rough and hot and smelly, but they were going somewhere. They were going to the Negev, the south country, the land of sunshine and flowers. And to the Christian, this old world is a desert. It isn't easy riding. It is a struggle. It is hard. But I have tried to picture them as they encamped. I can't imagine Rebekah's leaving the servant. I don't think she said to the servant, "You stay here and I will join you down the way." I don't think she went out to investigate the weird scenery of

the desert, the cacti and the desert flowers. I don't think
she was led astray by a mirage. I don't think she said,
"Oh, what a lovely field! I will meet you down in the south
country. Let me go out here and investigate this beautiful
scenery. Oh, what a lovely view!" I don't think she rushed
out after a mirage and grasped after something that faded
when she reached after it. But there are so many Christian
people who say to the Spirit of God, "I will meet you down in
the south country. I will meet you in Heaven. You go your
way and I will meet you in Heaven. I will take this course.
There is something lovely, there is something beautiful."
And they rush out after some little worldly something that
fades away and leaves them baffled. The person who tries
to feed himself on things of this world, who tries to be thus
satisfied, is rushing after mirages. When he lays hand upon
something that seems to be tangible and takes it and feeds
upon it, he is never satisfied. It stimulates and animates
his desire and makes him want more and more and more
until his very soul is on fire with the fire of Hell and he is
left empty. All that the world has to offer does not amount
to a thing.

She Followed Her Guide

I think Rebekah was satisfied to stay in the path that was
mapped out by her guide. The Spirit of God is our Guide;
He is our Teacher. I think I can see them as they stop to
camp in the evening. The sun has just gone down and the
western sky is ablaze. I hear her as she says, "Tell me
again the story you told me last night—how he was offered
as a sacrifice on a mountain. Oh, he must be wonderful! I
have never seen him but I love him! I love him now! And
do you mean all of that wealth is mine? I am his joint-heir?
Oh, I am so eager to get there! Let's leave early in the
morning, Eliezer. Let's not waste more time! I want to
see him." That is the spirit of the true Christian.

More about Jesus would I know,
More of His grace to others show.
. . . .
Spirit of God, my teacher be,
Showing the things of Christ to me.

Christian friends, we are on our way to the south country, the land of sunshine and flowers. "And Isaac went out to meditate in the field at the eventide: and he lifted up his eyes, and saw, and behold, the camels were coming." We are on our way. The camels are going. Our Isaac, the Lord Jesus Christ, may appear at any moment in a field of blue, just above the clouds and we will leave the camels and fly to meet Him. And oh, the unbounded joy that will flood our spirits then. "We know that, when he shall appear, we shall be like him; for we shall see him as he is."

X

The Second Coming of Christy

"And if I go and prepare a place for you, I will come again, and receive you unto myself; that where I am, there ye may be also."—John 14:3.

A Sublime Truth

One of the most sublime truths revealed in the Bible is that Jesus Christ is coming back to this world. Yes, the lowly Nazarene who trod the hills of Judea and the shores of Galilee more than nineteen hundred years ago is coming back. Do you find that hard to believe? Some people find it altogether incredible. That is because they do not believe that He actually went away. Some who aver their faith in His resurrection believe that He arose merely in the hearts of His disciples. Some believe that His Spirit arose but something happened to His body such as the soldiers claimed, 'While we slept His disciples came and stole Him away.' What good is a man's testimony if he was asleep?

"If I Go"

Jesus said to His disciples, "And if I go and prepare a place for you, I will come again." So the credibility of His coming back rests upon the fact of His going away, the fact of His resurrection and ascension coupled with His statement, "I will come again," and the credibility of His word. As to His going away there is no better established fact in ancient history than the resurrection of Jesus Christ. Neander Kaiser said, "There is greater proof that Jesus arose from the dead than there is that Augustus Caesar ever lived."

The Risen Christ Tangible

One commentator wrote concerning Jesus' explanation to Mary in the garden after His resurrection, "Touch me not; for I am not yet ascended to my Father," that Jesus could no longer be touched, that while He was living in this world He could be touched but now that He was gone He was no longer tangible. This is not an honest treatment of the text. Jesus told Mary not to touch Him because one was not to touch the High Priest as He was carrying out the functions of His office. He had left the altar, the cross, but had not gone into the Holy of Holies before the Father's throne. Therefore, He said, "Touch me not; for I am not yet ascended to my Father, and your Father; and to my God, and your God" (John 20:17).

Post-Resurrection Ministry

Apparently Jesus ascended to the Father immediately, then returned for His post-resurrection ministry. That afternoon He appeared to two men on the road to Emmaus and expounded the Old Testament so that their hearts burned within them. That same day in the evening Jesus appeared to ten of His disciples who were gathered in the upper room. They made the same mistake the commentator made but they were honest about it. "They...supposed that they had seen a spirit" (Luke 24:37). "And he said unto them, Why are ye troubled? and why do thoughts arise in your hearts? Behold my hands and my feet, that it is I myself: handle me, and see; for a spirit hath not flesh and bones, as ye see me have" (Luke 24:38,39). Does that sound like Jesus was no longer tangible?

He cooked breakfast for seven hungry fishermen one morning. That was no hallucination. When seven rugged men who have been pulling nets in the sea all night long are satisfied with an imaginary breakfast that is no hallucination! Jesus appeared to the disciples in the upper room and said to Thomas, who was absent the first time he appeared

to the group and who had said that he would not believe unless he could put his finger into the nailprints in His hands
and place his hand into His riven side, "Reach hither thy
finger, and behold my hands; and reach hither thy hand, and
thrust it into my side: and be not faithless, but believing.
And Thomas answered and said unto him, My Lord and my
God" (John 20:27,28). Jesus was seen after His resurrection by more than five hundred people at one time.

Eyewitnesses

Not only were there all of these eyewitnesses to His resurrection but there were also eyewitnesses to His ascension. Luke tells us in the first chapter of Acts that Jesus
"shewed himself alive" to "the apostles whom he had chosen...by many infallible proofs," and that He was assem-
bled together with these apostles. He tells us that after Jesus had given instruction to these apostles they were to
tarry in Jerusalem until they received the promise of the
Father, that they would receive power after the Holy Ghost
was come upon them and that then they should be witnesses
unto all the world. Then Luke tells us, "And when he had
spoken these things, while they beheld, he was taken up; and
a cloud received him out of their sight" (Acts 1:9).

Christ Is Now in Heaven

Now, my friends, if Jesus Christ arose from the dead,
(and there can be no doubt in my mind that He arose) and if
He appeared to Mary and said, "Touch me not," and to two
men on the road to Emmaus and expounded the Scriptures
until their hearts burned within them, and to ten disciples
in the upper room and said, 'Feel Me and see that it is I,'
and to doubting Thomas and caused him to doubt no more,
and if He ascended to Heaven, He is in Heaven now.

Did Not Die in Heaven

Jesus Christ did not conquer Death here in this world and

then go to Heaven and pass away up there. He did not go up there and die after threescore and ten years. He did not stay up there a hundred years, nor five hundred years, nor a thousand years, nor nineteen hundred years and then die.

He Liveth Forever and Ever

The Apostle John, looking with anointed eyes into the future in the Revelation, said, "And every creature which is in heaven, and on the earth, and under the earth, and such as are in the sea, and all that are in them, heard I saying, Blessing, and honour, and glory, and power, be unto him that sitteth upon the throne, and unto the Lamb for ever and ever. And the four beasts [cherubim] said, Amen. And the four and twenty elders fell down and worshipped him that liveth for ever and ever" (Rev. 5:13,14). Now if the Lord Jesus Christ is alive up in Heaven, now, it is not incredible that He shall come back here. He said that He would return. In the light of all of this I cannot by the wildest stretch of the imagination think of anything so incredible as that He should fail to come back.

His Coming Literal and Bodily

The second coming of Christ will be literal and bodily. When He ascended into Heaven the disciples stood on the Mount of Olives looking up where they had seen Him last as He appeared to them "like a tiny twinkling star in the broad daylight," before "a cloud received him out of their sight." They must have stood there for a long time before two angels stood by them and said, "Ye men of Galilee, why stand ye gazing up into heaven? this same Jesus, which is taken up from you into heaven, shall so come in like manner as ye have seen him go into heaven" (Acts 1:11). "This same Jesus"—the One who died on the cross, the One who arose from the dead, the One who appeared to Mary and said, "Woman, why weepest thou?" the One who appeared on the road to Emmaus and said, "Ought not Christ to have suffered these things, and to enter into his glory?" the One who appeared on the shore of Galilee and said, "Simon, son of Jonas, lovest thou me more than these?"—"this same Jesus" shall so come as He went into Heaven.

Personal

His coming will be in His own Person and does not refer to the coming of His other Self, the Holy Spirit, at Pentecost as some teach. It was, of course, after the Holy Spirit came at Pentecost that the Apostle Paul was inspired by the Holy Spirit to write, "For the Lord himself shall descend from heaven with a shout, with the voice of the archangel, and with the trump of God" (I Thess. 4:16).

Premillennial

The second coming of Jesus Christ will take place before the millennium. Now, let us see, what is the millennium? *Mille* means "thousand." *Annum* means "year." "Millennium" means "a thousand years." There will be a thousand years of righteousness on the earth. The prophets looked down through the annals of future time to a golden day, the millennium, a thousand years of justice and peace.

Age of Peace

There will be a golden day. "The wolf also shall dwell with the lamb, and the leopard shall lie down with the kid; and the calf and the young lion and the fatling together; and a little child shall lead them" (Isa. 11:6). This is a picture of peace. The Scripture does not say that a little child shall sing a song or quote a verse of Scripture in Sunday school. Of course, children may do this and that is fine, but this Scripture does not mean that. It means that a little child shall lead a lion, and the lion will not harm the child, because peace will prevail in the world. "And the cow and the bear shall feed; their young ones shall lie down together: and the lion shall eat straw like the ox" (Isa. 11:7). Think of it! Peace in this world! Even the ferocious and carnivorous lion shall be as docile and tame as a kitten and shall "eat straw like the ox." Peace! No war in all the world!

Man Powerless to End War

While this world is under the curse of sin it is impossible for men to avert war permanently. War began when Satan rebelled against God. No sooner was man created than Satan attacked God by striking at man, for he was a special object of God's love. There has been war in the world from that day to this. War is a diabolical institution with a diabolical origin and purpose. It will cease only when Jesus Christ comes and casts Satan into the bottomless pit. Man cannot end war because he cannot defeat Satan, who is the source of war.

Human Government

God instituted human government and in so doing He said, "Whoso sheddeth man's blood, by man shall his blood be shed." The same law which says, "Thou shalt not kill" provides the death penalty for those who kill. Government has a God-given right to take life. Of course, God will deal with governments for the misuse or abuse of this right. As Christians we are exhorted to be subject to civil authorities, for the "powers that be are ordained of God." And until Jesus Christ returns to put all things under His dominion there will be wars and rumors of war.

Survival of the Fittest

A scheme to discredit the Word of God hatched in Germany, and Higher Criticism, so-called, was born. The philosophy of the "survival of the fittest" brought forth its fruit—and the world was soaked in blood. A "war to end wars" was fought, a war to "make the world safe for democracy." It was a righteous cause: and through suffering and tribulation nations were brought to God. The aggressor nations were vanquished and there was "peace on earth" again. But it was not a durable peace. It was man-made peace. A League of Nations was formed and over the door of the Peace Palace were inscribed the words, "Peace and Safety." But "when they say, Peace and safety, then sudden destruction cometh upon them, as travail upon a woman with child" (II Thess. 5:3).

Third Reich

Out of the same Germany that produced the Second Reich came a Third Reich, a murderous Nazi Germany with her *Mein Kampf* and her hatred of the Bible, with her racial prejudice and her cruel persecution of the people to whom God promised, "I will bless them that bless thee, and curse him that curseth thee." This Nazi Germany, in a mad, ruthless campaign to crush the freedom from liberty-loving and peace-loving peoples, ran amuck among the nations of Eurasia. Free people were forced to fight. It was a righteous war. Backslidden Britain, apostate, atheistic Russia, and sin-loving America, so far from the God of our Fathers, joined in an effort to bring enduring peace. A price had to be paid. They suffered for their freedom or for their sins, but they fought a righteous war! Wars will come and fight we must! This is so whether they be wars of containment such as Korea and Vietnam or global wars such as Armageddon yet to come. Man is as powerless to end war as he is to stop the wind from blowing or the sun from shining.

Jesus Will Change Things

Do not call me a pessimist. I tell you, when Jesus comes, He is going to change things. "And he shall judge among the nations, and shall rebuke many people: and they shall beat their swords into plowshares, and their spears into pruninghooks." They will not need these instruments of war, for "nation shall not lift up sword against nation, neither shall they learn war any more" (Isa. 2:4). Peace! World peace!

Why? Because Jesus is going to reign, and He is the Prince of Peace.

Curse Taken Away

The curse that is now on the world will be taken away when Jesus comes. When Adam and Eve ate the fruit from the forbidden tree in the Garden of Eden God not only placed a curse upon the fallen pair and upon the serpent, but He said to Adam, "Cursed is the ground for thy sake." When God said that, in my imagination I can see luxuriant gardens turn to wildernesses. I can see verdant valleys as they become deserts. Thorns appear upon rosebushes, and all nature begins to groan and travail under the curse of sin. But when Jesus comes that curse will be removed.

"The wilderness and the solitary place shall be glad for them; and the desert shall rejoice, and blossom as the rose. It shall blossom abundantly, and rejoice even with joy and singing: the glory of Lebanon shall be given unto it, the excellency of Carmel and Sharon, they shall see the glory of the Lord, and the excellency of our God.

"Strengthen ye the weak hands, and confirm the feeble knees. Say to them that are of a fearful heart, Be strong, fear not: behold, your God will come with vengeance, even God with a recompence; he will come and save you. Then the eyes of the blind shall be opened, and the ears of the deaf shall be unstopped. Then shall the lame man leap as an hart, and the tongue of the dumb sing: for in the wilderness shall waters break out, and streams in the desert. And the parched ground shall become a pool, and the thirsty land springs of water: in the habitation of dragons, where each lay, shall be grass with reeds and rushes.

"And an highway shall be there, and a way, and it shall be called The way of holiness; the unclean shall not pass over it; but it shall be for those: the wayfaring men, though fools, shall not err therein. No lion shall be there, nor any ravenous beast shall go up thereon, it shall not be found there; but the redeemed shall walk there: And the ransomed of the Lord shall return, and come to Zion with songs and

everlasting joy upon their heads: they shall obtain joy and gladness, and sorrow and sighing shall flee away."—Isa. 35.

This beautiful chapter, in which every verse is a precious promise from Almighty God, has never been fulfilled. There is going to be a golden age when Jesus comes. "Behold, the days come, saith the Lord, that I will raise unto David a righteous Branch, and a King shall reign and prosper, and shall execute judgment and justice in the earth. In his days Judah shall be saved, and Israel shall dwell safely: and this is his name whereby he shall be called, THE LORD OUR RIGHTEOUSNESS" (Jer. 23:5,6).

Amillennialists

Now there are different views about the millennium. There are the amillennialists (so called because *a* is the Greek negative), who do not believe there is to be a millennium. At least a fifth of the Bible is prophecy pointing to such an age. The amillennialist must either spiritualize or ignore altogether such passages of Scripture as those cited above.

Past-Millennialists

There are those who hold that the millennium began about the time of Constantine and continued for a thousand years. There is nothing to support this view. The Catholics believe this to be a golden age because Catholicism flourished at that time. History teaches us that these centuries were the "Dark Ages."

Now-Millennialists

There are some who believe that we are living in the millennium now. We shall not take time or space to deal with this obviously unfounded and unsubstantiated view.

Postmillennialists

The postmillennialists have the idea that the world will grow better and better until gradually a golden day will dawn and after the millennium Jesus will return to find a converted world waiting for Him. There are two groups of postmillennialists—modernists and those who hold to the deity of Christ. The former group of postmillennialists are by far the more numerous. They do not believe in the literal, personal return of the Saviour. They do not really believe that Jesus arose and went away. They believe that He arose in the hearts of His followers and that He will gradually return through the Christianizing of society. They preach the "social gospel." The latter group of postmillennialists have been greatly influenced by the former groups but adhere to the resurrection and ascension of Jesus and, therefore, to His personal return. They believe that all the world will be won to the Lord and that Christ will return and find a converted world waiting for Him.

Premillennialists

I, personally, am a premillennialist. I believe that Jesus will come before the millennium. I do not see how there can be a millennium of peace without the Prince of Peace. We read in Revelation 20:6, "Blessed and holy is he that hath part in the first resurrection: on such the second death hath no power, but they shall be priests of God and of Christ, and shall reign with him a thousand years." If those who have part in the first resurrection are going to reign with Christ during the thousand years, the first resurrection must take place before the thousand years. It is clear that the first resurrection takes place when Jesus comes. He must come before the thousand years.

In Matthew 24:37-39 we read, "But as the days of Noe were, so shall also the coming of the Son of man be. For as in the days that were before the flood they were eating and drinking, marrying and giving in marriage, until the day that Noe entered into the ark, And knew not until the flood came, and took them all away; so shall also the coming of the Son of man be." Jesus is coming in a time when things are like they were in the days of Noah. Therefore, He will not find a converted world waiting for Him. Many other passages of Scripture make it obvious that His coming will be premillennial.

The Great Tribulation

When Jesus comes and takes His own out of the world there will follow a seven-year period, the last half of which is known to Bible students as the Great Tribulation. The Angel Gabriel told Daniel that "the prince that shall come" (that is, the dictator of the revived Roman Empire) would "cause the sacrifice...to cease" in the midst of the seven-year period (Dan. 9:26,27). It would appear that the Jews, back in their homeland, will set up their ancient altar and begin sacrificing again as they did two thousand years ago and they will begin this with a seven-year treaty entered into with them by the dictator of the revived Roman Empire and that in the very middle of this period the dictator will break his word and stop their worship of Jehovah. Now Daniel writes, "And for the overspreading of abominations he shall make it desolate" (Dan. 9:27). Jesus said,

"When ye therefore shall see the abomination of desolation, spoken of by Daniel the prophet, stand in the holy place, (whoso readeth, let him understand:) Then let them which be in Judaea flee into the mountains: Let him which is on the housetop not come down to take any thing out of his house: Neither let him which is in the field return back to take his clothes. And woe unto them that are with child, and to them that give suck in those days! But pray ye that your flight be not in the winter, neither on the sabbath day: For then shall be great tribulation, such as was not since the beginning of the world to this time, no, nor ever shall be. And except those days should be shortened, there should

*no flesh be saved: but for the elect's sake those days shall
be shortened."—Matt. 24:15-22.*

World's Worst Times

In our wildest imagination we cannot begin to visualize
the horrors of this awful period that is sure to come upon
this world. The curtain may go up at any moment on the
first act of the drama. Think of it! This will be the worst
time the world has ever known or ever shall know. It will
be worse than the great flood in Noah's day, worse than all
the wars of history, worse than the Spanish Inquisition, or
the French Revolution, or the Commune; worse than the
horrors of the Dark Ages. The Great Tribulation is going
to be worse than when men were pulled asunder by horses;
worse than when Christians were thrown to the hungry lions
on the sands of the arena to amuse the sadistic emperors of
Rome and their debauched cohorts. It will be worse than
the reign of Nero, or Marcus Aurelius, or Decius, or Valerian, or Diocletian. In the days of Decius Cyprian wrote,
"The whole world is devastated." The reign of Valerian was
worse and the reign of Diocletian was worst of all.

Hell Breaks Loose

The Great Tribulation will be worse than when people
were dipped in pitch and burned as torches. It is to be a
time of war, and famine, and death, and persecution, and
hatred, and fear, and fire, and hail, and thunderings, and
lightnings, and storms, and earthquakes such as the world
has never known. It is to be worse than Hiroshima and
Nagasaki. Satan will have unhindered sway over the world.
The bottomless pit will be opened and all Hell will break
loose on the face of the earth. God will pour out the wine
cup of His wrath upon the world.

Battle of Armageddon

This dreadful period will culminate in the bloodiest battle
in all the ages, the Battle of Armageddon, when blood will

run up to the bridles of the horses in the Valley of Jezreel. "Immediately after the tribulation of those days shall the sun be darkened, and the moon shall not give her light, and the stars shall fall from heaven, and the powers of the heavens shall be shaken: And then shall appear the sign of the Son of man in heaven: and then shall all the tribes of the earth mourn, and they shall see the Son of man coming in the clouds of heaven with power and great glory" (Matt. 24: 29,30). Christ shall reign on the earth on a literal throne in Jerusalem, and the golden glory of God will fill the earth as the waters cover the sea.

Drama in Two Acts

The second coming of Jesus will be in two phases. It is one great drama in two acts. The first act of the drama begins with the coming of Jesus for His people. The second act will begin seven years after the first act opens. The second act is the coming of Christ with His people. In the first act He comes in the air and the saints are caught up to meet Him. In the second act He comes to the earth and sets up His millennial throne and reigns for a thousand years.

Seven Years

I have stated that there will be a seven-year interval between the beginnings of the acts of this great drama. In Revelation the duration of this period is set forth in the very number of months and of days that elapse between the two phases of His coming. Also, in the ninth chapter of Daniel God sets forth in prophecy seventy weeks in which certain things were to be accomplished. These are weeks of years and not days. Literally "seventy sevens." One of these weeks, which is a period of seven years, is yet in the future and will take place just before Jesus comes "to bring in everlasting righteousness."

Signs of the Times

All of the signs of the times that we hear so much about

point not to the rapture of the church, but they point beyond the rapture to the revelation or glorious appearing of Jesus. The signs of the times point to the second act of the drama. There are no signs relating to the first act. However, the fact that signs are pointing toward the second act makes the first act, or the rapture, more expectant because, of course, the first act preceded the second one by seven years at least.

His Coming Imminent

The second coming of Jesus is imminent. It is liable to happen at any time. Jesus may tarry. I do not say dogmatically that He is coming soon. He may come very soon. I expect Him to. He may not. Nobody knows when He will come. We are charged to watch for Him. Do you expect Him to come today, or tonight? You do not? "Watch therefore...for in such an hour as ye think not, the Son of man cometh."

The Devil

At the close of the millennium the Devil, which shall have been bound during the thousand years, shall be loosed for a little season. He will go about like a roaring lion seeking whom he may devour, and will cause a stormy sunset at the close of the golden day. This will be a time of testing, but God will lay hold on the Devil and cast him into the "lake of fire and brimstone, where the beast and false prophet are, and shall be tormented day and night for ever and ever." After Satan is cast into Hell the wicked dead are raised and judged at the great white throne judgment. After this the "City Foursquare" with its jewel foundations, its gates of pearl, and its streets of flashing gold will come down from God out of Heaven. The eternal order begins at this time.

Watch for Jesus

Now Jesus has been here and He said He was coming back.

He told us to watch for Him. He said that we should pray, "Thy kingdom come." Do you really want Him to come soon? Suppose that right now as you are thinking on this subject Jesus should come. Would you meet Him in the sky? Would you be caught up with the hosts of others to meet the Lord? You may be ready if you will. That is why Jesus died. He would not have toiled and struggled under the burdens He carried. He would not have been crowned with thorns, and spit upon, and cursed, and mocked, and laughed at, and scourged, and crucified, if He had not wanted to see you saved. Thank God for Jesus Christ! Thank God that He came into this world, and thank God that He is coming back. He said, "I will come again."

He Said He Would Return

A little boy followed his mother to the gate one day and said, "Mother, please take Bobby."

"No, Bobby," she said, "I cannot take you because I am going to the hospital for an examination. I might have an operation. I do not know when I am coming back, but I am coming back. I will come on the train. When you hear the whistle blow remember that Mother might be on the train."

That evening the train whistle sounded and little Bobby was out in the yard with a bound. "Daddy, Mother's coming! Mother's coming!" he cried.

"How do you know, Bobby?"

"Well, she said she was coming when the whistle blows."

But she did not come. The next day the whistle sounded and once again Bobby ran to meet his mother, but she still did not come. But Bobby said, "I know she is coming. She said she was." One day, sure enough, she came back. Oh, my friend, Christ is coming! Christ is coming! You say, "How do you know?" I know because He said He would. Will you be ready when Jesus comes?

$2.29 Economy Series

(Clothbound; by Dr. John R. Rice, unless indicated)

Any 5 copies for $10.50

Any 10 copies for $19.00

Plus postage of 5%

A KNOW-SO SALVATION
ALL ABOUT CHRISTIAN GIVING
AMAZING POWER OF THE GOSPEL IN PRINT
"AND GOD REMEMBERED"
BREAD FROM BELLEVUE OVEN (R. G. Lee)
"COMPEL THEM TO COME IN"
COWBOY BOOTS IN DARKEST AFRICA (Bill Rice)
ETERNAL RETRIBUTION (W. E. Munsey)
GOD'S CURE FOR ANXIOUS CARE
GREAT AND TERRIBLE GOD, THE
HELL IS NO JOKE (R. L. Sumner)
HOW TO OBTAIN FULLNESS OF POWER (R. A. Torrey)
I LOVE CHRISTMAS
IMMANUEL: "GOD WITH US"
JOHN 3:16 (Moyer)
KISSES OF CALVARY (Jack Hyles)
LET'S STUDY THE REVELATION (Jack Hyles)
RIGHT WAY IN MARRIAGE (Cathy Rice)
ROMANCE AT RED PINES (Elizabeth Handford)
SEEKING A CITY
WE CAN HAVE REVIVAL NOW
WHEN SKELETONS COME OUT OF THEIR CLOSETS
WORLD'S MOST POPULAR GAME, THE (Parker)

Order from your bookseller or from

SWORD OF THE LORD PUBLISHERS
Box 1099, Murfreesboro, Tenn. 37130

LET'S BUILD AN EVANGELISTIC CHURCH

By Dr. Jack Hyles. The next best thing to following step-by-step in the tracks of probably one of the most successful soul-winning pastors of our day. Through the pages of this book you may follow the famed pastor of the great First Baptist Church of Hammond, Indiana, as he builds a visitation program; as he finds prospects--and wins them to Christ; as he witnesses in public places, in hospitals; in his church at invitation time; as he wins souls with his family plus many other most helpful suggestions. 144 pages. $2.50

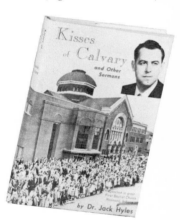

KISSES OF CALVARY and Other Sermons--10 in all--are messages given just as preached in the pulpit of the great First Baptist Church, Hammond, Indiana, by Dr. Hyles, the pastor. Such sermons as these are responsible for an average of over 30 decisions per Sunday for the last year or more. 155 pages, pictures of Dr. Hyles, his mother and his church. . . . $2.29.

Let's Use Forms and Letters

In response to persistant demands for the same, Dr. Jack Hyles has compiled this collection of Forms and Letters used in the ministry of First Baptist Church of Hammond, Indiana. Not a book of stirring sermons; not sweet devotionals; not a profound commentary on the Scriptures. Invaluable suggestions as to workable apparatus to assist in the development of great soul-winning churches. Every pastor and S. S. worker will want a copy! Practical. 116 large pages, hard bound, $3.00.

SWORD OF THE LORD PUBLISHERS
Box 1099   Murfreesboro, Tennessee

The Home: *Courtship, Marriage, and Children...*

During twenty-four years of pastoral, evangelistic and editorial work, Dr. Rice has been confronted with troubled folk of all ages, in private conversation, in letters by the thousand, and in forums, with questions on courtship and petting, child discipline, family altar, birth control, duties of husbands and wives, divorce, normal sex life in marriage and many other home problems. Thus he saw the need for a sane, biblical, understanding and practical book on the home and problems of married people. We believe he was eminently qualified to write it—by his experience, his deep and and burning devotion to the Lord, his undoubted Bible scholarship and his skillful writing.

An excellent wedding gift; every home should have a copy, every young person. Family record, marriage certificate. 22 long chapters, 381 pages in lovely cloth binding.

America's Best-Seller on Prayer

200,000 Printed

The miracle-working God still answers prayers as He did in Bible times and for our fathers. Here one can learn how to pray in the will of God, grow in faith, really get things from God and live the joyful life of daily answered prayer. Commended by hundreds.

HYMAN J. APPELMAN says: "Last night I finished your marvelous book on Prayer. I say advisedly it is the very greatest thing of its kind I have ever read . . . Thank God for the Holy Spirit's using you to write every line of it."

Attractive paper jacket, beautifully cloth-bound, 328 large pages, 21 chapters.

Sword of the Lord Publishers
Box 1099, Murfreesboro, Tenn. 37130

All About Christian Giving

by Dr. John R. Rice

Here is the clearest, most complete examination ever made of the Bible teaching on giving. It is not a book to get money or primarily on the Christian duty to give to the Lord's work. Rather it is an examination with heart-warming illustrations of God's promises to those who put Him first in every way.

Dr. Rice proves that tithing is for Christians today, but that the "storehouse" idea in tithing is an Old Testament principle only. He gives practical, sensible teaching on the mechanics of tithing.

COMMENTS:

Dr. Bob Jones, Jr., President, Bob Jones University:

"This is a book that will shatter the chains which selfish ecclesiastics have forged to bind and enslave some of the dearest saints of God. The plan of giving outlined here is scriptural, and any Christian who follows it will find a new joy in his giving."

Dr. V. R. Edman, President, Wheaton College:

"Clear, concise and earnest counsel on what the Bible teaches about our giving, and the joy and blessing that accompany such stewardship."

Beautiful two-color cover, 174 pages

Paper-bound $1.00 - Hardbound $2.29

Order from your bookseller or from

SWORD OF THE LORD PUBLISHERS
Box 1099, Murfreesboro, Tenn. 37130